Leading Remote and Virtual Teams

Managing yourself and others in remote and hybrid teams or when working from home

by Kevan Hall and Alan Hall

Version 1 January 2021. Published by and © Global Integration Ltd 2021

Global Integration Limited
2 Wellington Business Park
Dukes Ride, Crowthorne
Berkshire, RG45 6LS
United Kingdom

+44 (0)118 932 8912
europe@global-integration.com
www.global-integration.com

Contents

Contents

Part I Introductions

Chapter 1. Introduction

In 2020 we experienced a sudden and unexpected global experiment in remote working. Driven by the need to keep our people safe, and our businesses running, organizations around the world sent millions of people home to work.

If your boss had asked you in January 2020 to put together a project to move half of your people to work from home, how long would you have estimated that that would have taken to implement? It turns out the answer for most organizations was about four days.

Prior to COVID-19, approximately 4% of full-time employees worked from home, by mid-2020 40% did. McKinsey estimates that 20% of people are likely to work remotely at least part of the time in the future.

Remote and hybrid working, where people alternate between working in the office and working remotely, are not new. Working from home was the norm before the industrial revolution. Modern remote working enabled by communication and computing technology has been increasing progressively since the early teleworking experiments of the 1970s. Salesforces have worked this way for decades.

Kevan developed the world's first commercially available remote and virtual teams training in 1994. Since then, we have trained over 100,000 people in more than 400 leading organizations around the world in the skills of working remotely. We have had the opportunity to learn what really works and test out tools and ideas in a wide range of cultures and industries.

Before COVID-19 the research was very positive about remote working – it led to better performance, higher levels of autonomy, higher engagement, and lower levels of stress. Remote working was seen as an attractive perk.

Many individuals and organizations have had some positive experiences working from home even during the COVID-19 lockdowns. They appreciated being able to keep their families safe and balance outside commitments with work. They enjoyed the autonomy, stayed productive and very few people missed their morning commute.

However, there were consistent concerns about loneliness, wellbeing, mental health, and social isolation.

It would be rather unfair to blame all of this on remote working.

It is a very different experience choosing to work from home under normal circumstances and being forced home with your family to avoid a global pandemic and then juggling work around your other commitments. **Experienced remote worker, Financial Services, USA**

Gallup found that pre-COVID-19 people who worked from home full time were 40% less likely to always or very often feel burned out at work than people based in an office. By mid-2020, people working from home felt 12% more stressed than people still in the office.

As we return to a more normal situation, we should expect remote working to return to a more balanced and positive experience.

Remote working will not be available to everybody. McKinsey estimates that in emerging economies such as India, Mexico, and China, only between 12% and 21% of workers can do their work remotely for three to five days per week without losing productivity. For many European countries and the US, that jumps to nearer 30%.

Remote working will be unevenly distributed across industries and roles. Some industries, like finance and insurance, professional services, and IT and communications, are just more suited to remote working. Others like agriculture, hospitality and construction are less so. Management and professional roles will become more remote than manufacturing, accommodation providers and food service.

This book is aimed at the people lucky enough to be in the category of people who can work wholly or partly remotely.

Most people able to work remotely have now overcome the initial challenges of getting set up to work from home and learned to connect to their remote colleagues.

Many companies that were previously reluctant to let people work from home, including some of the leading technology companies, have learned that their people usually become more productive. They have learned they can trust their people to work hard and that there are significant reductions in the costs of offices and other facilities.

It will be much harder to argue that people cannot work from home now they have proved that they can. Companies' resistance to remote working, often founded in out-of-date notions of control has been undermined or eliminated.

As people got a little more used to working from home, we found that the conversations we were having with many thousands of people on live web seminars quickly shifted to reflect a huge desire to connect, discuss their experiences and maintain community and relationships.

Leading organizations started to focus more on the wellbeing of their people. Those that did it well, experienced an increase in employee engagement even during a very difficult period, and established a leadership legacy that will pay off in the long term. Those that did it badly will find it difficult to recover their leadership credibility.

But it is not all positive. Some individuals have struggled with remote working, work life balance and boundaries between home and work. There are lingering concerns about how we maintain relationships, onboard new people, manage performance, stay visible and creative, and maintain the wellbeing of people when we meet less often.

Some managers have struggled with their need to control people and supervise work. They wonder how they can manage performance in the future.

We need to equip individuals, teams and leaders with the mindset and toolkit needed to overcome these challenges.

Everyone expects an increase in remote working to remain after the pandemic. If McKinsey's estimate is accurate, and 20% of the workforce will work remotely for most of the time, this would be about five times more people than before the pandemic.

This will have enormous implications for the way we lead, collaborate and work. It will have implications for society including the future of cities, transport congestion, consumer spending, and carbon emissions. Our focus will be on the impact on ways of working, skills, and corporate culture.

If we ask people in our training programs what they would personally prefer for the future, most would like to work from home for three or four days per week. Surveys before the pandemic showed that people who work this kind of pattern tend to be the most engaged of all employees. Our clients currently seem to be expecting people to be able to work remotely between two and three days per week, we will see how this develops.

This hybrid working pattern may give us the best of both worlds, giving us the flexibility of working from home for a period and the opportunity to meet face-to-face with our colleagues from time to time to focus on collaborative work and maintain relationships.

We believe that the move to home and hybrid working has the potential to be better for both individuals and organizations. Managed well it can lead to higher levels of autonomy, lower cost, higher engagement, more resilience, and improved access to talent.

Many of our clients are taking this opportunity to re-examine their ways of working. They understand that now we need to move from remote and hybrid working being an emergency measure to it becoming a sustainable long-term pattern of work.

In some cases, our clients have already re-designed jobs or whole business models that used to rely on high levels of face-to-face contact with colleagues or customers, such as sales or consulting. Many have seen a rapid acceleration in the digitalization of their business processes and customer experiences – this is unlikely to be wound back in the future.

This book moves beyond the basics of remote management to help build a sustainable way of working. It builds on 25 years of experience training people to work this way. There are some new lessons that came out of the lockdown experience but many of the fundamentals have been very consistent over that time.

As leaders become more familiar with working remotely, they are starting to recognize that many aspects of leadership and management happen without much planning or effort when we are in the same location. Without the free by-products of proximity, we need to be much more explicit and intentional about building relationships, managing visibility, and building community.

When we work with organizations making changes to their way of working, corporate culture, or organization structure, we always say that there is "no such thing as a free lunch". You make some choices. These choices give you some advantages and cause you some new problems.

Organizations have already seen significant benefits from having more people working from home. First and most importantly, they have been able to keep many more of their people safe and at work during a global pandemic.

As things start to stabilize, organizations are realizing opportunities to

- improve productivity
- raise engagement
- lower facilities and other costs
- get access to a broader pool of talent

Cost savings are always popular and apply both to organizations and individuals.

- according to PGI news, the average office and facilities saving for employers is $10,000 per employee working remotely per year
- according to TECLA, a global IT recruitment company, remote workers save around $7,000 per year from reducing the cost of commuting, food, clothing, and childcare

Many organizations remain concerned with factors like

- how can we exercise control in this more distributed environment?
- will collaboration be as effective?
- what will be the impact on our people's wellbeing?
- can we maintain creativity virtually?
- how do we manage performance when people are working remotely?

The benefits are compelling, but we do need to overcome the concerns to make this way of working sustainable.

Our participants tell us they experience a range of advantages and challenges when working remotely.

Advantages for the individual	Potential challenges
<ul><li>Higher engagement</li><li>More autonomy and flexibility</li><li>Lower commuting and work costs</li></ul>	<ul><li>Less social contact, harder to get to know new colleague and build trust</li><li>Work life blurring and balance</li></ul>

Advantages for the individual	Potential challenges
• Location independence • Fewer distractions on individual work • Less sickness absence • More inclusive meetings • Broader range of employment options • More learning from working on multiple teams	• Out of sight out of mind – staying visible • Less spontaneous communication • Less feedback and recognition • Too many virtual meetings • More switching between multiple tasks and teams

Our job as leaders is to deliver the benefits and manage or eliminate the potential challenges.

The good news is that none of these challenges are insurmountable. We have spent the last 25 years finding tools and solutions to manage all of them.

This book will give you lots of ideas, practical tools, and coaching questions to help you and your colleagues deliver the benefits, overcome the challenges, and develop a sustainable pattern of work that works for you as individuals and for the organization as a whole.

The book is also a reflection of our own long-term working reality. Our company Global Integration has been "virtual first" for over 25 years. For the first 15 years, we did not have any office locations. We have both spent most of our careers at Global Integration working from home and spend most of our time either training or managing people who work remotely.

Kevan worked in major multinationals in human resources, business planning, manufacturing operations and geographic expansion. He often worked in international roles requiring high levels of travel and remote working. He founded and runs a "virtual first" global training organization with people based around the world.

Alan's early career included field-based and account sales management with broader sales and marketing management experience in major multinationals. Since joining Global Integration, he has trained many thousands of people around the world in remote working, matrix management and agile working.

Together we are going to focus on the things that we have found people struggle with most in working remotely.

We are also trainers. We do not like to identify a problem without giving people some practical solutions, so we are going to share some practical ideas, tools and tips that have worked for tens of thousands of people from many of the world's leading organizations.

- Part II of the book is about **managing yourself.** If you are a manager working from home or in hybrid teams, you will need to develop your own sustainable system of work and manage your own wellbeing. The concepts and tools in these chapters also make great coaching topics for you to discuss with your people

- Part III focuses on **collaborating with others virtually** from fewer better virtual meetings to mastering multiple team membership, managing the expectations of others, and succeeding in hybrid teams

- Part IV is about **staying visible and connected when we are apart** – focusing on visibility, networking, and communication

- Part V moves on to consider **leading other people remotely** – from adapting your leadership style to finding the right balance of trust and control, running positive remote performance conversations, and managing inclusion and creativity

In each chapter, we will leave you with some coaching questions that you can use to reflect on your own situation and to coach the people in your teams.

Our intention is to give you the toolkit to build a way of working that is both more productive for the organization and more sustainable and engaging for you and the other people who work there.

If you need help doing this for your team or organization, we run highly interactive workshops and web seminars for leaders, intact teams and individuals based on these principles. You can see more free web seminars, videos and other resources or contact us through www.global-integration.com If you like the book, you will love our training programs.

We wish you good luck
Kevan and Alan

Chapter 2. Deciding what work to do where?

I spend part of my time working from home, part based in one of our regional branch offices, I go into the office once every two weeks to meet with my team, and I use a coworking space near to home if I want to get a bit more social contact. **Marketing Manager, Insurance, Poland**

In remote and hybrid teams we can perform our work in a range of different locations. We need to think about how this will change the way we work and if we are working in different home and office locations, which work is best performed in which location.

In organizing your work when working from home or in hybrid teams, it is important to start by being clear about the type of work you need to perform. There are three subtly different concepts here that enable us to think systematically about what kind of work is best delivered from which locations.

These were some of the earliest ideas that we brought into our remote teams training over 25 years ago and remain an essential foundation for virtual success.

The three concepts are

- individual and collective work – how do we perform our tasks
- asynchronous and synchronous working – when and how do we need to coordinate with others
- star group and spaghetti team working – how do we organize collectively for coordination or collaboration

Individual and collective work – how do we perform our tasks

Before COVID-19, research on remote working consistently showed that individuals working from home were more productive.

In a mid-2020 survey of more than 12,000 workers in the US, Germany and India, management-consulting firm Boston Consulting Group found that productivity could be maintained in a virtual or hybrid work setting even in lockdown situation where distractions were higher than usual.

- 75% of employees said that during the first few months of the crisis, they had been able to maintain or improve their perceived productivity on **individual tasks** (such as analyzing data, writing presentations, or executing administrative tasks).

- 51% of people said they had been able to maintain or improve their productivity on **collaborative tasks** – things like working in teams and interacting with clients. Still a majority but not as positive.

By organizing our work around what is best delivered individually from home and what we need to do collaboratively with others we can get the best out of each mode of work.

The things we do outside of meetings are usually individual work. Individual work needs to be coordinated so we are aligned and heading in the same direction but does not require intensive collective collaboration.

What parts of your role can be delivered individually, and which require you to collaborate with groups of other people?

Asynchronous and synchronous working – when and how do we need to coordinate with others

When organizing our remote or hybrid activity, it is also useful to think about when and how we need to coordinate with others.

- In asynchronous working, we do not necessarily need to be available at the same time or the same place as our colleagues. We do our own individual work and then forward it to the next person in the chain or complete our portion of the work ourselves. Most people report being more productive at asynchronous working when working from home.

- In synchronous working, we need to be available at the same time, even if not the same place to do live collaborative working. This means getting face-to-face or in live virtual meetings. Synchronous working is generally more difficult to deliver remotely.

We often compare this to the difference between being part of a relay team and a rowing team. In a relay race, we focus on our own performance and the handover to the next individual. In a rowing team, we are all in the same boat at the same time and need to coordinate closely to stay in rhythm and generate the best speed for the boat overall.

The more you can organize or break down your tasks into things that can be delivered asynchronously, the easier it is to deliver remotely.

A lot of our collaboration is on shared documents on Google Docs. We can all work in parallel and add our contributions at a time that is convenient to us. We rarely need all to be there at once. **Project Manager, Aerospace, France.**

Conversely, do not use your synchronous time for things you can do asynchronously.

I was asked to fly from Singapore to Shanghai for a team meeting. When we got there, we watched a video and then flew home, what was the point of that? **Customer Service Manager, Healthcare, Singapore**

Star group and spaghetti team working – how do we organize collectively for coordination or collaboration

If you read our previous books Speed Lead, Making the Matrix Work, or Kill Bad Meetings, you will already be familiar with the idea of star group and spaghetti team working. It is a useful way of thinking about how we organize ourselves in virtual working.

It came from our very early realization in our remote teams' training that synchronous, collective, traditional teamwork where people are deeply interconnected and interdependent (what we call spaghetti teamworking) was relatively difficult to deliver remotely.

Sometimes, of course, we need this intensive form of teamwork, so it is essential that we learn to be brilliant at it. However, we have learned that people spend a lot of their time together working on tasks that do not require this intensive teamwork and could more easily be delivered individually or asynchronously.

If we can learn to focus our collective, synchronous time only on the spaghetti topics we can have much more engaging and productive meetings and save a lot of time.

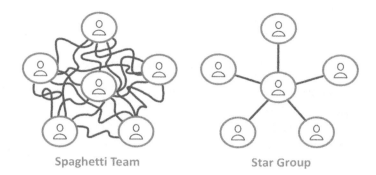

Spaghetti Team   Star Group

Star group working is a hub and spoke pattern where individuals do their own work but are coordinated and aligned by reporting to the same boss.

When people are working in star group mode

- People normally work on individual objectives
- Roles do not overlap
- People have unique skills
- Communication is relatively infrequent
- People can normally complete their daily work without information or service from others in the group
- Work may be passed on from one member of the group to another
- Information is shared for learning and interest

All these characteristics make this work very suitable for working from home.

Communication during this way of working tends to be one-to-one and can usually be done through technology or individual calls.

Spaghetti team working is a deeply interconnected way of collaborating where everyone is connected to everybody else.

When people are working in spaghetti team mode

- Objectives require the cooperation of all members of the team
- Individual roles overlap
- People have complementary skills
- Communication is relatively frequent
- People are dependent on others in the team to get their daily work done
- Information is shared to get things done

Communication during this way of working needs to be synchronous and normally happens in live face-to-face or virtual meetings.

We are not, of course, saying you need to choose to be one or other of these ways of working for 100% of the time. All teams spend some of their time working as a star group and some of their time working as a spaghetti team.

The secret in productive working from home and hybrid working is to be clear about what mode you are in and organize accordingly.

The biggest mistake is to get people together collectively in meetings and discuss topics that could more easily be delivered individually or through technology. We will show you how to avoid this in the chapters on virtual meetings.

We have a regular daily stand-up meeting where we all get together and listen to a series of individual status updates. There is nothing much I can do with this information as our roles are not interdependent. It is only relevant to the individual and our manager. The rest of us are sitting waiting for our turn. **Agile Team Member, Packaged Goods, Netherlands**

Putting the 3 concepts together

If we bring these 3 ideas together, they give us some consistent guidelines on how to organize our virtual and hybrid work

Better done from home	Easier in an office or requires virtual meeting capability
• Individual Tasks • Asynchronous work • Star Group work	• Collective tasks • Synchronous work • Spaghetti Teamwork

- When performing individual, asynchronous, and star group tasks, all the evidence suggests that most people are even more productive when working from home where we normally have fewer distractions and an increased ability to focus. The more we can organize our tasks into this way of working, the more effective we will be when working remotely
- When performing collective, synchronous, or spaghetti team tasks
  - If we are working in a hybrid team, we should cluster our most collaborative tasks into a time when we can be together
  - If we are working completely virtually, we need to improve our virtual collaboration skills and ways of working

o Whether working in our face-to-face or virtual meetings, we need to make sure we do not spend time on tasks that could be delivered individually or asynchronously

What is the best hybrid pattern for your team?

Determining the right pattern of work for your specific team depends on two key factors

- the nature of the work you are performing, and particularly the collaborative aspects of that work
- individual preferences on working location and times and how much your corporate culture is willing and able to accommodate these

Personal preferences

Different individuals with different family responsibilities at different stages in their life will have different preferences as to working location and hours.

In *Resetting normal: defining the new era of work*, a global study of 8,000 participants conducted by Adecco. Researchers found that employees on average want to spend nearly 50% of their week working remotely, with 75% of them feeling it was important to maintain flexibility over their working schedule.

We need to be aware of and discuss personal preferences as an input to deciding what hybrid way of working works for our team.

We may need to revisit this conversation as the team membership changes. We probably need a facilitated process for determining the right pattern.

This process needs to be consistent with any boundaries that have been put in place due to the corporate culture of your organization and any other constraints such as regulation. It is important to be clear about any limits to flexibility before opening this discussion or we could set expectations of flexibility that we are unable to deliver.

Coaching question

- How can we combine the needs of the work and our personal preferences into a hybrid working pattern and schedule that works for both?

Part II – Managing yourself

The move to a new way of working gives us an opportunity to redefine our roles to find the right balance between being productive and developing a sustainable pattern of work that works for us as individuals.

This is relevant to everybody, as an individual this is an opportunity to help define a way of working that meets your personal needs and preferences.

If you are a leader, you can have a big impact on your team and yourself by modelling these behaviors and using the principles to drive coaching conversations to ensure that your people are doing the same.

If we want to grasp this opportunity, we need some ideas and tools to address some of the common challenges.

We also need to take ownership; we cannot expect other people to define how we will work in our own homes or what works best for us as individuals. We need to develop our own preferences and communicate and negotiate these with the people we work with, and sometimes with our families or housemates too.

In this section, we will focus on 3 common challenges in working from home

1. Managing boundaries and transitions between home and work, and work life balance

2. Designing your pattern of work – practical strategies to both sustain productivity and manage renewal

3. Managing your own wellbeing when working from home

Chapter 3. Managing boundaries and transitions between home and work

"You would not sleep at your desk; you should not work from your bed."

When working from home, the boundaries between work and home can become blurred, and this can lead to overwork, distraction, role conflicts, and a lack of organization.

However, this same blurring can also give us more flexibility and autonomy and enable us to develop a system of work that is more tailored to our individual preferences and needs.

How you manage this is highly personal. Someone with family or caring commitments may prefer a very different pattern from someone living alone.

This has, of course, been much more difficult to manage during the COVID-19 lockdowns than during working remotely in normal times. People and families have been forced together in close proximity for long periods, and this has caused additional challenges. If you have survived this period, then normal remote working is much easier.

It is your life and your home – nobody else can control the detail of your work time or how much you integrate or separate your home and work lives.

Only you can take ownership and set your own routines and boundaries. You should not expect or want others to do it for you.

You are also not designing a system to suit hundreds of people, just you, so this can be very personalized, around the needs of your job, of course.

Some aspects of the way you manage boundaries are entirely within your control. Others you will need to negotiate with your colleagues or any people you live with.

It starts with understanding the challenges and deciding what is best for you.

There are three primary challenges in setting and communicating boundaries when working from home

- Managing role transitions
- Setting boundaries in space
- Setting boundaries in time

Managing your transitions

*"At work, I am normally hard driving and assertive, I tend to get straight to the point and push for completion fast. It has made me successful in my job, but unfortunately, that does not work out so well for me at home." **Sales Manager, Logistics, Australia***

Without boundaries between our work and home roles, we can experience blurring of the two roles, which can lead to confusion and conflict when we move from one to the other. We create boundaries naturally to simplify and organize our lives, but when working from home we inherently have more opportunities for work and home roles and tasks to interrupt each other.

Many of us experienced the increased blurring of roles during the COVID-19 lockdowns with family responsibilities and work responsibilities competing for our attention during work hours, and work being on our mind in the evenings and weekends. As the situation stabilizes an important part of sustainable home working is having boundaries between home and work that work for you personally.

Some people have very contrasted or segmented roles, where they act very differently at home than they do at work. Just about every TV cop show includes a storyline about their difficulty separating their work role from their home life.

It can be hard to make the switch from being, for example, an assertive, fast paced, results driven person at work to something more relaxed and caring at home.

Other people experience much more role integration where there is relatively little contrast between their identities at work and home. The bigger the difference between your roles, the larger the psychological transition you need to make when moving between them if you want to avoid one role blurring into the other.

We will return to the theme of what works better for you personally – work life separation or work life integration later when we consider work/life balance.

When we move from home to a traditional office in the morning, it looks like this.

- Exiting the home role – getting dressed, following our morning routines, saying goodbye
- Movement and transition – commuting to work, moving to a new location, thinking about the day ahead and what you need to get done, and beginning the transition to the other role

- Entering the new role – arriving in the new location and role, engaging with colleagues, setting up our work

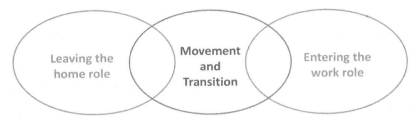

These phases, and the reverse when going home in the evening, enable us to manage our role transitions. We have time to prepare psychologically for the other role, and this helps prevent unwanted blurring – where we bring our problems, stresses, and behaviors from one role into the other.

Perks such as on-site leisure, sporting, or childcare facilities which were intended to help can make this worse by encouraging further blurring. Parents who bring their children to on site crèche facilities, for example, can report feeling more distracted and more guilty about the proximity of their children.

People normally have rituals, habits and routines that signal each of these phases. What are (or were) yours?

I stand in the same place every day to get on the train, I see the same people at the same times. I use the time to listen to podcasts and maybe clear my inbox if I am busy. I do not miss the hour a day traveling each way, but I do miss that time to myself to reflect and reset. **Marketing Manager, Banking, UK**

It can help to try to replicate the previous patterns you had as nearly as possible as these were ingrained patterns that signaled work/non-work to yourself.

"Even when I work from home, I still get dressed every day for work. I go out to the front door and take a short walk before starting work, it is a signal to myself that I am now at work. I do the same at the end of the day" **Finance Manager, Energy, Mexico**

Take a moment to reflect on how you move from one role to another.

Coaching questions

- What were your routines and habits when going to work in an office?
- What routines do you have when working from home?
- What do you most miss?
- How could you recreate what you miss when working from home?

Replacing the commute

A major benefit of working from home and something that few people miss is the time spent commuting.

"Marchetti's Constant" is the fact that the average commute, from the time of ancient Rome to today has stayed constant at around half an hour each way. As transport has improved, we have just increased the distance between our home and work.

It seems, on an average, people prefer not to commute further than 30 minutes each way. However, for some, it is a much bigger chunk of their day, particularly if we are commuting into a major city.

"By the time I have driven to the station, caught the train and the underground to the office, and returned in the evening I spend nearly four hours a day traveling."

"Why would you choose to do that? "

"It is the quality of life out here in the country"

Interview with a commuter at a train station on BBC Radio. UK

A study by Harvard and New York University economists comparing 2 x 8-week periods before and after the lockdown found that people working from home spent around 48 minutes more time per day connected to their offices, eating into the time saved from commuting.

According to a different study by the Becker Friedman Institute for Economics at the College of Chicago of people working from mid-March to mid-September, the average return commute before the pandemic was 54 minutes. During lockdown

- 35% of the time saved was spent working
- 15% was spent on household chores
- 11% was spent on childcare
- 4% went to second jobs
- 30% was spent on leisure

However, in this study, they also found that total overall working hours **substantially declined** from 36.4 hours to 32 hours. This indicates that people were spending more time on non-work activities during their day.

You may have found that the blurring of roles was beneficial during this unprecedented period, enabling you to look after different commitments and to switch the timing of your work around to cope.

"People appeared to be working longer hours. But employees said they were carving out pockets of personal time to care for children, to grab some fresh air, exercise, or walk the dog. To accommodate these breaks, people were likely signing into work earlier and signing off later." **Microsoft internal study of workplace analytics, mid 2020.**

If you find it challenging to separate your home and work roles, or if this blurring is causing you problems in either place, then you should think about your routines and transitions to help make the separation clearer, psychologically if not physically.

If you consciously choose to start work a little earlier, finish work a little later and make time during the day for other family or social commitments, then provided that is OK with your work colleagues, that is great.

If you find you are working all the time and cannot switch off, then this is unlikely to be sustainable. It is important to make conscious choices about this rather than drift into a pattern of working that is unhealthy and probably unproductive.

If you enjoyed the walk to the station, 30 minutes reading, planning your day, calling a colleague, or catching up on social media – do something similar for a short period before you start and after you finish work.

You probably also did these things at a routine time – to catch a particular train, miss the worst of the traffic, or work around family commitments. Sticking to the same times can make the transition easier.

If you always wanted to take more exercise, taking a walk, or something more strenuous, is a great way to reset your mind as you move from work mode to home mode and back again.

Coaching questions on managing transitions

- Do your home and work roles interfere with each other?
- Do you regularly bring problems from work to home or vice versa?
- How much of your time have you saved by not commuting? How have you used this time?
- What do you miss about your commuting time?
- How can you manage your transitions from home to work more effectively?

This can be a good discussion to have with the people you live with. They may be better placed than you to see where your role gets blurred and what problems this brings. You will also need their support in implementing any changes you need to make.

Setting and communicating boundaries in space and time

There is nothing hard-and-fast about the boundaries you set – they can be highly individual, so it is essential to negotiate and communicate these boundaries. For example, people who choose to send emails outside working hours are often surprised when others complain they feel they need to respond immediately, and it interrupts their evening – in most cases, the sender never expected an immediate response.

This is even more critical if you are in a leadership role. In Alan's first corporate role, it was an unsaid expectation that he remained in the office until after his manager had left for the evening. If we translate this to a remote environment, it can become challenging if those boundaries are not set and communicated, and team members feel they are "always on".

Successful remote workers and leaders establish boundaries in space and time that separate their work and non-work activities.

Boundaries in space

These represent the boundaries that mark out the place where you work. In a traditional office this is easy, we dress differently, move to a different place, and usually have a defined space to work in. At the end of the day, we leave all that behind and return home.

In working from home, some people are lucky enough to have a separate office where we can still close the door at the end of the day. Most have dual use spaces using kitchen tables or desks fitted into bedrooms or crammed under the stairs.

"You cannot drive away from the office at the end of the day when it is in your house. The three priorities you did not get to today are feet away from you. Why not go back to the desk and polish off one more task before bed?" **Corporate Lawyer, Automotive, Canada**

If we are not clear about establishing these physical spaces and when to use them, it is very easy to get drawn into working outside normal hours

Here are some tips on managing the physical boundaries around being at work when working from home.

- Have a regular agreed physical workspace

- Try to keep the equipment, papers, files, or other boundary markers that define your workspace from spilling out beyond this space
- Avoid clutter – research shows that constant reminders of disorganization can increase our stress and reduce our ability to focus. That annoying clean desk policy at work may be a good idea at home. Fans of Marie Kondo, which both of us have in our families, will be delighted
- If you cannot close the door on this area, have a clear agreement on how and when you will pack your work materials away at the end of the day
- When you are working, try to restrict access to others to the space to minimize interruptions
- Get dressed, it signals to yourself if no one else, that you are now at work
- Have separate devices such as different phones for home and work and leave them in separate places

Coaching questions

- How do you mark out your space for work?
- How do you stop it from being too accessible outside normal working hours?

Boundaries in time

Instead of being driven by the needs of nine to five office work and the schedules of public transport or driving time, now we have an opportunity to think about what working times best work for us personally and for our roles.

Here are some ideas.

- Set your starting and finishing times – make a routine and stick to it, negotiate this with and other people you live with, and hold each other accountable
- Take regular breaks and organize your day – see more on this in the next chapter
- Manage interruptions from your other roles - have a signal or barrier that indicates when you do not want to be interrupted
- Agree when you are available and how quickly you will respond. Will you be dealing with messages outside of work time?
- Turn on "out of office" or "away" notifications when you do not want to be disturbed. Do not check your work devices for emails, messages, and alerts outside working hours
- Schedule time in your diary for personal commitments. If you need to pick up your kids from school or have other commitments, then block in the time so people can see you are not available

"When we had our first lockdown in the UK, I was dealing with work alongside home-schooling my children. I was happy to work into the evening so I could take some time with my children during the day. However, when I sent emails after 6 p.m. I scheduled them to be delivered at 9 a.m. the following morning. This highlighted to the team I managed that they were not expected to work late just because I chose to". **VP, Consumer Goods, UK**

In 2017, French employees gained the "right to disconnect", from work emails outside working hours. Companies with more than 50 workers are obliged to draw up a charter of good conduct, setting out the hours when staff are is not supposed to send or answer emails.

If you work with international colleagues, you need to be aware of this. A legal approach gets in the way of much of the flexibility we recommend for individuals to define their own pattern of work (but it is not optional if it exists). It is worth having a discussion with your colleagues around how you will handle your time boundaries.

Coaching questions

- What are the rules that will work for you, your colleagues, and your household to support the boundaries between work-time and home-time?
- How do you organize your time boundaries?
- What gets in the way and causes you to break these boundaries? How can you manage this?

Boundaries in space	Boundaries in time
• Physical workspace • Equipment, papers, files, or other boundary markers that define your workspace • Restricting access to others to the space • Getting dressed • Separate devices for home and work • Self-imposed rules and routines	• Starting and finishing times • Breaks • How you organize your day • Managing interruptions from your other roles • Scheduling the need to coordinate your time with others • Dealing with messages outside of work time

The Boundaries Audit

If you manage a team, this is a good topic for a collective discussion. It is an opportunity for individuals to share their personal needs and what works for them and discuss and agree on a set of norms that work for the individual and the team.

Use the coaching questions on role transitions and boundaries above to structure the conversation. Discuss

- What is working well?
- What changes do we need to make to sustain this way of working for the long term?
- What causes us to stray outside of our boundaries?
- How can we support each other in this?

In collaborative work, we are constrained by the need to coordinate our time with others, so these boundaries need to be explicitly negotiated. You may also have time commitments where you need to be available to customers or colleagues, and you will need to work around these.

It is much easier to be flexible about when people perform their individual tasks. Start there when you look for more time flexibility.

Work life balance or work life integration – your choice

In finding the right work life balance, we have found it useful to distinguish between two different concepts

- work life integration – how much overlap is there between work time and non-work time
- work life balance – is the total time allocated to work and non-work activities OK for you

Work life integration

Some people choose to separate roles and prefer a clear dividing line between life and work. This prevents blurring and keeps the roles distinct. If boundaries are clear they are easier to enforce, but you may lose the benefits of flexibility.

A clear separation is more helpful when your home and work roles are very different and the transition between them is difficult to manage.

Others see benefits in more integration. We all appreciated the ability during the lockdown to take time during the normal working day to meet personal and family commitments. If we spent a couple of hours on this during the day, we may have needed to spend some time working in the evening to catch up. That seems fair to us.

It is easier to work this way when your work and home roles are more similar (transitions are easier) and you have more control over your working pattern.

Some people prefer this type of working when work time and family time are intermingled. As we have seen above, this does lead to more blurring of the boundaries, but this may be OK for you.

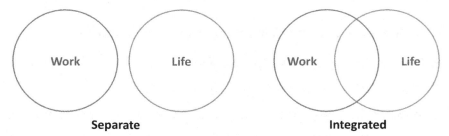

Separate   Integrated

Benefits of work life separation	Benefits of work life integration
• Prevents blurring • Prevents role conflict • Boundaries are easier to enforce	• Gives more flexibility to shift work hours around • Helps us work around other life commitments
• Easier when work and home roles are very different • More necessary when your job requires a lot of coordination with others	• Easier when home and work roles are more similar • Easier when you can schedule your own working time

We work in a business where several family members are actively involved. We often find business discussions sit naturally alongside family events and we are generally happy with that as we are all very engaged with the success of the business. However, we also make sure that we make time to focus on family only issues or business conversations can become all-consuming, and rather boring for those who are not so directly involved.

We may each accept a different balance of work and home time, depending on the stage of our career, our personal circumstances, and our personalities.

The important questions are – does the level of integration work for you? If not, what are you going to do about it?

Coaching questions

- Where does work life integration or separation work for you right now?
- What are the challenges?

- What can you do to change the level of integration to something that works better for you?

Work life balance

When people talk about work life balance, usually they feel that they are working too much. We cannot remember any participant on one of our training program over the years who complained about having too much life.

The key questions with work life balance, therefore, are how can I be more effective in the time I have available, and say no when the workload becomes too much?

We are not talking here about emergencies or exceptional circumstances. Most people are prepared to put in extra hours if the situation is critical. The problem is if long hours become our normal working routine.

We will give some ideas in the next chapter on how to find the right balance between being productive and finding a sustainable pattern of work.

Coaching questions

- What is your work life balance like right now? Does it work for you?
- What is your target? What balance would you like to achieve?
- What specifically stops you from getting there?

Chapter 4. Design your most productive and sustainable working pattern

I managed to maintain my productivity in the early period of working from home by just working harder and longer. I was also worried about my job when the lockdown period ended. As I got used to it though, I realized this was going to be a long-term thing and I needed to get a better balance. **HR Business Partner, Professional Services, Spain**

After an initial period of compulsory working from home, many organizations are now planning for a future where flexible working becomes the norm for many more people. To make this successful we need the skills, way of working and culture to make flexible working sustainable for the long term.

Before COVID-19, research on remote working consistently showed that individuals working from home were more productive. From Chinese call center workers to US professionals people tend to be significantly more effective working from home, largely because of improved individual engagement, fewer distractions, and a better ability to focus.

In a 2020 survey of more than 12,000 workers in the US, Germany and India, management-consulting firm Boston Consulting Group found that productivity can be maintained surprisingly well in a virtual or hybrid work setting. The survey also shows that there is a significant appetite for flexible ways of working among employees, as well as increased openness to this from managers

The evidence suggests that we can be significantly more effective at performing individual tasks from home and maybe even slightly more effective on collaborative tasks.

Nevertheless, there remain concerns that some of this productivity is being bought at the expense of longer working hours (though the evidence of this is mixed). As we move into a more normalized pattern of remote working, we need to ensure that we balance productivity with sustainable ways of working for the longer term

Sustainable productivity

There are several principles that can help us develop a sustainable routine for working productively at home. This is about finding a balance between our need to be productive and our need to renew our energy. We can do this by organizing our pattern of work to deliver both.

These principles need to be tailored to your own preferences, attention span, role, and preferred ways of working.

We will introduce several concepts then look at how you can apply them in a sustainable and productive system of work that works for you personally.

Knowing the rhythms of your day

Most people move through recurring 90 to 120-minute periods or cycles, known as ultradian rhythms, both during the day and while sleeping.

During daytime, our alertness increases in the first 60 minutes of this cycle then starts to decline.

Somewhere between 90 and 120 minutes into the cycle, the body starts to want some form of rest or recovery.

The symptoms that we are starting to need a break include yawning, a desire to stretch, hunger, tension, procrastination, difficulty concentrating, or making more mistakes.

If we can organize our day around these cycles, we can take the benefit of the improved periods of attention and ensure we allow for enough renewal to allow us to continue to be productive later in the day.

Coaching questions

- How do you experience these rhythms?
- What is a good attention span for you when focusing on your work?
- How can you tell when your attention is wandering?

Chunking your work

Chunking means creating 25-minute work sprints followed by 5 minutes of break or doing something fundamentally different. This is sometimes known as the pomodoro technique, and you can find timing apps for your phone based on this.

This chunking can significantly improve our ability to complete work, whilst at the same time embedding a routine of breaks and renewal. It has been shown to improve focus, stop procrastination and encourage task completion.

Each chunk focuses on a discrete task or group of similar tasks that you can complete in that time.

It is important to turn off any distractions during these short sprints.

I have started to cluster together all those short "keep in touch" client emails into 30-minute chunks. Because they are a similar type of task, I seem to get through far more of them in that time rather than when I spread them across the week. I also have far fewer alerts popping up to remind me to do them. **Sales Associate, Utility, Brazil**

Research has found that processing e-mails three or four times daily is the most productive pattern, though this will vary depending on your role and requirement to be responsive.

How can you chunk your deliverables or groups of smaller similar tasks into 25-minute chunks?

Seeking flow

Flow is that state of concentration where we momentarily forget everything else. This is sometimes called being "in the zone" or in a "flow state".

In his studies on work behaviors, Mihaly Csikszentmihalyi focused on above average rather than true peak performance. He found that, at work, people felt they were confronting above-average challenges and using above-average skills, about half the time, (which is what you would expect mathematically).

Managers reported themselves in this flow state more often – about 64% of the time. Clerical people were in a flow state about 51% of the time and blue-collar people about 47% of the time they were at work. It seems that the more challenging and broad ranging your job, the more you are likely to experience flow.

Flow is a very positive experience. People report feeling strong, active, creative, concentrated, and motivated.

Csikszentmihalyi found that people rarely reported that feeling of flow during leisure activities – only about 18% of their leisure time. There is a paradox here. People are more motivated and challenged at work than during leisure time. They are also more likely to report feeling apathetic during leisure time. However, when asked, most people prefer to spend more time at leisure.

If we want to experience the benefits of flow, there are some practical things we can do to increase the probability that we will get into and stay in "the zone" by creating the three elements of flow state.

- Choose a task that is at or just above your current ability level
- Organize the work so you get immediate feedback (at home you may have to give this feedback to yourself)
- Minimize distractions

If we can learn to encourage periods of flow state to focus on important activities, then we can be more productive without working for longer

Coaching questions

- When have you been in that situation when you really felt as though you were in the zone, things were working well, you were really focused and not easily distracted?
- What stops you from getting into or staying in a flow state?
- How can you recreate that state more regularly?

Different times for different tasks

There are some types of activities that use a lot of brain energy and resources – particularly prioritizing, future planning, and prediction.

These are particularly difficult because we are having to imagine something that does not exist yet and make some judgments about what is likely to happen in the future. These are both areas that require manipulating higher levels of uncertainty and use more of our brain capacity.

Once we know this, it makes sense to organize to do these kinds of activities when you have a fresh mind. Ideally, this is when you are rested, when you have had the right nutrition, and when there are relatively few distractions. We will come back to how you minimize distractions later in this chapter.

Schedule future-oriented planning work or creative thinking at the times that work best for you – perhaps early in the morning or after a break or exercise. Experiment to find what works best for you.

On the other hand, for most people, the lowest phase of our ultradian rhythms is somewhere between 3 and 4 p.m. A great time to take a break, re-energize, or do more trivial tasks. Maybe the traditional mid-afternoon naps in some cultures really were a good idea.

Visualize your work

One of the best things about our agile team is our Kanban boards. Current priorities are really visible, and I get great satisfaction from moving a task to the completed column. **Agile Team member, Software services, Hong Kong**

Many teams and organizations have experimented with techniques such as Kanban for making work visual, encouraging a focus on current work in progress, and driving for completion.

A simple Kanban board has three columns; pending, work in progress and completed. Tasks are written on post-it notes and put in the first column. We select our next priority and physically move the post-it to the work in progress column (Kevan sticks the current post-it on his PC screen).

We then focus on this task, and only this task, until it is completed, and we can move it to the final column.

To Do	In Progress	Done

There is something satisfying about physically moving post-its but you can also do this through apps or even a spreadsheet if that works better for you.

The beauty of Kanban is three-fold

- It encourages visibility – you can see what work is pending and where you are focusing right now

- It focuses us on work in progress – at any one time you are focusing on a single priority
- It encourages completion – you get a feeling of satisfaction by moving things to the final column, the brain loves to complete things

It seems to work better for many people than a long list of "to do" items.

Coaching questions

- How do you organize your action lists and work in progress?
- How can you use these ideas to improve?

Organizing for renewal

I used to almost feel guilty taking a break when I was working from home. I worried that my boss would think I was not working hard enough. I have learnt that I am much more productive if I take a short walk at midday. **Customer Service Manager, Facilities Management, Japan**

A lot of discussion about stress only focuses on a negative form of stress, technically known as distress. This form of stress can be very harmful. We hear a lot less about the positive form of stress which is known as eustress.

As with developing physical capability, developing mental and emotional capability requires us to push past our comfort zone for a period and experience eustress. Without eustress, we will not develop new capabilities or improve our resilience or performance.

However, even eustress is healthy **only** provided we balance this with sufficient recovery and renewal time.

Even with moderate levels of activity, as we have seen, we need short breaks or changes in activity within our 30-minute chunks.

After 90-120 minutes, we should aim for at least a 10-15-minute break to reenergize our brain and body and restore concentration.

To be effective at this we need a repertoire of break activities and the discipline to take the breaks.

To get you started, here are some ideas for different types of renewal activities for short and longer breaks.

Type of activity	In 5 minutes	In 10-15 minutes or longer
Physical	Desk yoga, stretches, stair walking, hydrate, and splash water in your face	Take a walk, make a walking phone call, learn to juggle
Relaxing	Slow breathing, stretches, mindful moments	Listen to guided meditation or music, watch something that makes you laugh
Social	Small acts of appreciation to colleagues and friends, have a virtual coffee	Call a friend or family, virtual lunch break

Type of activity	In 5 minutes	In 10-15 minutes or longer
Brain boosting	Learn and use a new word, listen to complex music, write something by hand	Do a puzzle, draw something, write a poem, take up painting, play a brain training game, or try a language app
(Occasionally) Clear something that drags you down	Organize your desk, unsubscribe from 5 emails you never read	Clear your inbox, organize your workspace

It is good to focus on break activities that are very different from the work you normally do. If you are a yoga teacher then do not choose a yoga break! Mix up the different types of activity and choose things you enjoy to give yourself variety and stimulation.

To add some randomness, why not give your ideas a number and roll a dice to decide which break activity to do next.

The second discipline is to make sure you take breaks. If you set a routine of 25-minute chunks and 90-120-minute cycles of work, then it is easy to set an alarm to remind you to take a break at the end.

Alternatively, set yourself a habit that every time you move something to the completed column of your Kanban board, you take a break.

If you have the kind of job where back-to-back meetings fill your day, then you may need to block in explicit renewal time, particularly at midday. On virtual meetings, you can often get away with turning off your webcam for a while and doing some standing or stretching.

Both of us use stand-up desks to keep moving during web seminars and meetings. They can also be a great way to differentiate one of your 25-minute chunks and help you get into a state of flow.

- What gives you renewal – in 5 minutes or in 10-15? Make a list of the things you enjoy, find relaxing and have access to in your home or nearby
- How can you organize to take your breaks?

Putting the 6 concepts together into a system of work that works for you

You can take these ideas and put them together into a system of work that considers the needs of your work and your personal preferences in how you like to organize your day. Here is a place to start.

1. Break your day into 90-120-minute cycles with breaks and renewal in between
2. Within each cycle organize your work into 30-minute chunks or sprints, write each of these chunks on a post-it and add it to the pending part of your Kanban board
3. When you start the chunk move it to the current WIP to make it visual
4. When you have finished a chunk, move it to the completed column and celebrate, take one of your 5-minute break activities
5. Set alarms on your phone for major breaks every 90-120 minutes and take one of your 10-15-minute (or longer) break activities

6. Focus future oriented, complex, or planning tasks early in the day

You should take this as a guide, tailor these principles to your own attention span, the nature of your work, and your working preference, design an experiment to try it out.

Coaching questions

- What pattern would work for you?
- What stops you from doing this?
- How can you ensure you take your breaks?
- How will you overcome these barriers?

Managing distractions

In an information economy, the scarcest resource is attention.

We all have access to huge amounts of information, but our capability to absorb it is limited.

Our focus allows us to pay attention to the most important and relevant information while filtering out the irrelevant.

This is not something that anyone else can do for you, particularly in your own home. We need to take personal ownership for managing our own distractions and attention when we are working remotely.

Unfortunately, some very smart people with massive resources are dedicated to creating distraction through social media and other channels – which are always potentially more interesting than what is happening at work.

At work, we are also creating more information than individuals have the capacity to consume. On average people receive over 120 incoming emails per day. During and after the lockdown periods increased use of tools like MS Teams or apps like Slack and Yammer have added to the volume of incoming messages. Every message is accompanied by a flashing notification or audible alert. When we click on it, we get a shot of dopamine to reward and reinforce our distraction.

Whereas previous working generations have struggled to get sufficient information to make decisions and to understand their business, today the challenge lies in sorting out what is relevant from a deluge of information.

Many people respond by trying to multitask. Some are even proud of their ability to do several things in parallel. In one survey, representative of the U.S. population, 93% of respondents thought they could multitask better than or as well as the average person.

Unfortunately, multitasking is a myth, what we really do is switch from one task to another and back again and do neither of them as well as if we concentrated. We are also less likely to complete tasks when we multitask.

You can find some amusing videos online on the impact of distraction – try searching for "Inattentional Blindness".

We also know that creative, receptive, and curious people are particularly susceptible to attempting to do multiple things at once. This may be part of what makes them successful by making them receptive to new ideas and experiences, but it can easily become an overdone strength.

The Four Stages of concentration and distraction

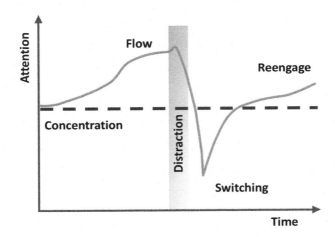

- **Examining the Nature of Fragmented Work** by G Mark, VM Gonzalez, J Harris found that people at work spend an average of 11 minutes working on a specific working sphere before switching to another one or being interrupted, and 57% of all working segments were interrupted before they were completed

- Gloria Mark at the University of California showed that where people frequently switch from one task to another, they feel they work harder but produce less. These people report significantly higher levels of stress, frustration, workload, and pressure

- A study in the **Journal of Experimental Psychology** found that students doing complicated maths problems were 40% slower when they also had to switch to other tasks

- Glen Wilson at King's College London studied 1,000 adults asked to do an IQ test who were then interrupted by emails and texting. They scored 10 IQ points lower. This is similar in impact to losing a night's sleep and more than twice the effect of smoking cannabis

- Finally, people asked to write a report took 50% longer to finish than those who did not switch between tasks repeatedly

All these studies show what we know to be true. That if we are constantly distracted, we do pay a price in impaired performance. Multitasking is a myth.

The Economist Intelligence Unit (EIU) paper "In search of lost focus" in 2020 found that the impact of distractions per person annually was the equivalent of 28% of total working hours and that fewer than 15% of responding organizations offered training to their people in how to cope with this major productivity issue.

David Mayer from the University of Michigan estimates that the time costs of switching are between 20% and 40% of potential efficiency for information workers. This means working more hours to complete a given task or getting less done in a given time.

- Only 55% of people resume the same work immediately after an interruption
- After interruptions, 40% of the time people cannot easily recall the previous task they were doing. They lose track and take time to find their place and rebuild the state of mind needed to resume

The research shows that 60% of interruptions are caused by external factors, and the biggest two external factors are other people, and technology.

In general working from home (in normal times) reduces people's distractions, though during lockdown family distractions were higher than normal.

Most people have, however, reported an increase in technology driven distractions – more calls and emails.

The EIU study found that the biggest source of interruptions (34%) was face-to-face interruptions from colleagues about work issues. When working remotely these interruptions tend to come by email or instant message.

A further 23% of interruptions came from peripheral distractions in the office such as ringing phones or chatty colleagues. This can happen if you have housemates also working from home.

During the lockdown, I and three of my flatmates were all working from home. It was very difficult when one or more of us was on a call. Even with headphones I sometimes had to take my calls from a cupboard. **HR Manager, Consulting, Finland**.

For individuals with families working from home, this can be replaced with (sometimes welcome) family distractions.

Working from home also brings a whole new set of potential distractions from the easy availability of food, TV, social media, and video games to the immediate demands of family and others in our households.

We do not need to be too miserable about this, some distractions give us welcome renewal and keep us productive. As Kevan was writing his part of a draft of this section, his 8-month-old grandson was "helping" wrap Christmas presents in the next room. Regular breaks were required to watch this. He also took the opportunity to upload a video of this to a family messenger group, thereby spreading the distraction more widely. Some distractions are too good to miss!

Dealing with technology distractions

People in most organizations deal with hundreds of technology-driven distractions per day, primarily emails, phone calls and social networking (or as we heard it called recently, "social not-working")

Here are some practical tips for managing the number of distractions through technology.

- Turn off the wireless connection to your PC and keep other technology like phones switched off at critical focus times. It is very hard once you are connected to emails and messages to avoid getting dragged off into reactive work. Try not connecting for the first hour of the day whilst you plan, focus, and prioritize

- Only check emails at set times. The EIU study found that 18% of people check their inboxes every few minutes, 70% check hourly. Depending on your role, the most effective frequency seems to be to check 2 or 3 times per day

- Set your status on any collaborative tools to "busy" or "away" and suspend alerts when you need to avoid distractions or, even better, close them down altogether

- Stay off social media and the internet except in breaks – it is designed to be distracting

How do you manage technology distractions?

Another approach is to organize our work to be more tolerant of distractions. Here are some ideas on how to do this.

- Set aside a whole day to work on a specific goal. Take the materials you need to a separate room or work from home. Stay there until you have finished.

- Have checklists for regular activities – even though you know what you are doing. In our case, when we are preparing a workshop, we tick the steps off a checklist – it means we do not need to use effort thinking and remembering all the steps and, if we are interrupted, we just go back to the next step on the checklist

- Work within your natural rhythms and make time for renewal. We are more easily distracted when we are tired, or our attention is starting to lag

- Create triggers for concentration in your environment. Mottoes, images, whatever catches your eye, and visual reminders of the need to concentrate on your priorities, such as the Kanban approach

- Set a routine for getting back to what you were working on quickly once you have been interrupted. When you are interrupted, take a moment to mark your place with a post-it note or position the cursor where you were working if you are doing something on a screen. Alternatively, make a quick note of what you need to do when you get back. These are all effective ways of resuming interrupted work more quickly

- Help others by giving realistic deadlines for their response to your emails, not everything requires an urgent response. This helps people avoid immediate distractions

Role-modeling from managers is extremely important here. In a remote environment, our participants frequently tell us they feel unable to switch off notifications or technology for fear of being seen as "away" and therefore ineffective – despite the reality being quite the opposite. Managers need to communicate that it can be appropriate to switch off, for example, MS Teams, if you are looking to get into a flow state.

We need to make clear that individuals will not be penalized for not always being online or available. People who have more autonomy to plan their work and discretion over their schedules can focus more strongly. Where possible, we should give people that autonomy to improve productivity.

Internal interruptions

The other 40% of interruptions are caused by internal issues. These are things going on inside our own head.

Our minds tend to wander when we trigger a memory, when tasks are routine and do not take up a lot of our processing power, or when things are boring.

We need to learn to veto those internal distractions, to head them off at the pass before they consume our scarce attention. We can do this through awareness and labeling.

The biggest challenge is to become **aware** when you are doing it quickly and return to your focus. Meditation is the most powerful mental skill we have come across for doing this. When we meditate, we learn to become aware of the fact that we are straying internally. Often just noticing it calmly can help defuse the internal interruption and remind us to go back to our original thing.

Labeling the internal interruption is also very powerful. Simply say quietly to yourself "interruption". If it is an emotional intrusion, you feel angry or frustrated about something, then labeling (calmly describing your emotional reaction or state to yourself) will automatically tend to defuse the reaction.

Labeling engages the rational part of your mind, which automatically suppresses the emotions.

Often just making ourselves explicitly conscious about the internal interruption is enough to help us go back to what we were trying to focus on.

Coaching questions

- How do you manage your distractions?
- What causes most of your distractions?
- How can you organize your work to control these distractions?

Setting new habits around sustainable personal productivity and renewal

Embedding changes to our working patterns require us to set new habits. What habits do you plan to implement?

In his book "Tiny Habits" B. J. Fogg gives some practical advice on establishing new habits.

1. Behavior change requires motivation – be clear about why you are doing it
2. It requires ability – are you able to do it. This can be increased through learning and practice or by getting the right tools and equipment. If something is hard to do, find ways to make it

easier — automate it, get organized, or start with a very small change that is easier to implement

3. Set a Prompt — to remind us to exercise the change. The best prompts are links to existing behavior or events that are already embedded

Fogg suggests using the format, "when I …., I will ……." and remembering to celebrate success when you do it.

- When I first sit down at my desk, I will work on my #1 priority for 30 minutes before looking at emails.
- When I make a cup of tea, I will stand up and make a sales call, or do 3 press-ups
- When my phone alarm goes, I will throw a dice and take the "winning" break
- Before I eat lunch, I will take a 10-minute walk

Start small and embed the habit, once it is working you can scale it up if needed.

Coaching questions

- What habits do you want to implement?
- How can you raise your motivation to change?
- How can you make it easier to do?
- How can you link it to a prompt or trigger behavior that you already do?

Only 28% of people working from home felt less focused than they did in the office. **Economist Intelligence Unit**

Overall, we think the ability to focus should be improved when working from home, particularly when working on individual tasks.

Chapter 5. Manage your own wellbeing when working from home

Working from home normally is quite peaceful. It is a very different experience from being unable to leave the house with two kids, my partner, and the dog, doing home-schooling, and trying to work at the same time. **Customer Experience Manager, Food Service, Sweden**

Many organizations expect that there will be longer-term fallout for their people from the COVID-19 period, particularly in terms of mental health and sustainable working from home practices.

It would be unfair to blame many of the mental health challenges of 2020 on remote working. It was a very stressful year for many people with concerns about their health and families, restricted living conditions, and an unending series of alarming press reports.

In normal times remote workers suffer lower levels of illness generally and are less likely to report feeling "burned out" than those who are office based.

Nevertheless, there are some valid concerns with sustainable wellbeing for people working from home without the right level of support.

Some organizations even reported an improvement in engagement over the lockdown period as people have felt that their wellbeing was being addressed and considered by their senior leaders. Many are keen to retain this more human face of leadership in the future.

In the past, when we worked face-to-face, there were many more opportunities to understand people's physical and mental states and much more bandwidth to have conversations and to help. If we are working more remotely, we need more explicit techniques as part of our management and collaboration toolkits to consider this.

There are also some very practical considerations. Alan's fitness tracker shows he covers around 10,000 steps per day when delivering a typical face-to-face workshop, and many more traveling before and after the session. If he does not leave the house and delivers web seminars all day, that falls to less than 1,000 steps. We need to replace the exercise we got from traveling to work with something else.

Some organizations have sophisticated wellness programs and offer specialist support in areas such as mental health. It is beyond the scope of this book and our expertise to get into great depth on this topic. If you are experiencing significant mental or physical health problems for any reason, then you should seek specialist advice. In this book, we will give a short, non-medical overview of some of the factors to consider when working from home.

Our experience in leading conversations about this topic is that many people already know what makes a healthy lifestyle, the challenge is in implementing this as part of your working from home routine.

Some key concepts

As we researched this content for our web seminars, we found most of the good literature and ideas seem to flow from the articles and books by Loehr and Schwartz or books such as The Corporate Athlete: by Loehr and Groppel.

They focus on four areas of wellbeing

1. **Physical** – nutrition, exercise, sleep, renewal, and physical energy
2. **Emotional** – intelligence, positivity, optimism, psychological wellbeing, managing energy, and emotional resilience
3. **Mental** – managing unhelpful thoughts and stress
4. **Spiritual** – which refers to secular and non-religious themes. The importance of such things as gratitude and appreciation, values, and our sense of purpose in life

Their approach came from a comparison between professional athletes and what they call "corporate athletes," – individuals striving for consistent, excellent performance over a long span of time.

When comparing corporate athletes to physical athletes, there was one key element that was crucial in sports and often missing in the corporate world —a holistic approach that emphasizes the body, the mind, the skills, and the spirit.

Loehr & Schwartz created a hierarchy called the "performance pyramid." Each of its levels – spiritual, mental, emotional, and physical—work together to create an overall healthy balance and effective performance.

Physical wellbeing

It is not that I do not know how to live a healthy lifestyle. It is just hard to do it when you get up early, commute to the lab, and work long days. **R&D associate, Environmental Services, Denmark**

Early research around the lockdown period suggests that it saw increased food prices, less dietary variety, lower levels of physical activity, and perceived weight gain. Physical activity will be a priority for many of us in the aftermath.

It is hard to say something about physical health without stating the obvious and being patronizing. There are no real secrets to this. If you have not seen any of many books, blogs, TV shows, or news items for the whole of your life, you might find the next list useful.

- Eat a balanced diet – including lean sources of protein, lots of fresh fruits and vegetables, and limited amounts of processed foods and added sugar
- Take regular exercise – you should get at least 30 minutes of exercise a day at least 5 times a week. Walking at a rapid pace is enough – if it gets your heart rate up. Any amount of physical activity is better than none
- Maintain a regular pattern of sleep – 7-9 hours of sleep per night
- Keep to a healthy weight

If you have a health problem that prevents you from doing any of these things you should seek professional advice.

Unless you have an underlying health condition the challenge is nearly always in motivation. We know we should take exercise and eat healthily but it is easier not to.

So, what is different about this when working from home?

- you do not naturally take as much exercise if you do not leave the house. It is easy to fall into a sedentary pattern, therefore the need to take some form of exercise is even more important.

- It is much easier to exercise. You never have the excuse that you did not bring your running gear, it is a few feet away in your cupboard. You saved an hour a day from commuting that you could use to take a walk or do some other exercise.

Our advice is to focus on your motivation and your habits

When he was in his mid-30s Kevan had his first ever rigorous medical in France as part of a new job. He was generally very healthy and always had high stamina but was overweight due to high levels of travel and spending more than half of the week eating in hotels and restaurants.

The doctor pointed out that keeping fit and keeping your weight down has nothing to do with how you feel in your 30s, 40s, or even 50s, it was all about the quality of the last 10 years of your life. It was something that stayed with him because, if you wait until you feel unwell it is going to be too late.

Exercise works best when it is a habit. Once you are into a routine it is easier to stick with it than to stop. Once you fall out of your routine it becomes easier and easier not to do it.

We both set diary alarms to remind us to do some exercise at least every other day.

Another simple approach is to use the "tiny habits" method from chapter 4. For example, "every time I put the kettle on, I will do three press ups". If you drink as much tea and coffee as we do that will soon add up.

Having a stand-up desk can make a difference. Alan covers over 2,000 steps delivering a 2.5-hour web seminar from his stand-up desk. This is time he would otherwise have spent sitting down. Simple changes to your working practices like this can make a significant difference over weeks or months.

There are many, many other books, blogs, videos, and TV programs available on this subject if you want to find out more about this.

It is also important to have the right setup at home. Very few organizations have looked into the ergonomics of people working from home. At Global Integration, we have an assessment to look at the health safety and environment of new home-based people. In particular, pay attention to a good chair, a decent sized screen, and the ability to vary your focal length between the two.

Coaching questions

- What stops you from doing the things you know lead to a healthy lifestyle?
- Where can working from home help you adopt healthier habits
- What gets in the way, and how can you overcome these barriers?

Mental, social, and emotional wellbeing

Again, we are not qualified to offer advice on clinical problems in these areas but can offer some general advice for most people working from home.

When we are working from home there are some additional challenges that can be caused by feelings of isolation and loneliness, by the difficulty in maintaining work relationships, and the need to socialize in a virtual environment. Here are some ideas that our participants have found helpful.

Isolation and loneliness

Loneliness does not come from having no people around you, but from being unable to communicate the things that seem important to you, **Carl Jung**

We have run web seminars for clients on dealing with social isolation and loneliness when working from home. This was a major concern in the early months of the lockdown.

There is a lot of literature that emphasizes the negative effects of social isolation on health, quality-of-life, stress, anxiety, and sleep problems. These normally come from studies of people suffering from long-term social isolation and feelings of rejection.

Neuroscience has now shown that the part of the brain that registers and reacts to social rejection is the same part that registers physical pain.

But 2020 was different. We found it was useful to frame the difference between being socially isolated by other people in a normal situation, which implies rejection, and the very different shared experience of social isolation due to lockdowns that we were all going through at the time. The latter was driven not by rejection but by supporting each other and our families' health and wellbeing.

Loneliness and a feeling of social isolation are both evolutionary mechanisms. Throughout most of human history, the riskiest thing that could happen to an individual was to be isolated from the group, so social isolation can trigger feelings of lack of safety

Individuals have very different responses to this and to cope with potential feelings of loneliness, we need to both

- create an environment where connections happen easily and regularly whilst being aware if individuals start to disengage
- have individuals take responsibility for connecting if they are not getting the social connection, they need

Short term loneliness is a signal that your social networks are lacking and is an evolutionary mechanism designed to motivate you to reach out and connect. Longer term, loneliness becomes a problem when self-reinforcing negative feelings about loneliness set in.

true

If this happens, then we can start to behave in a way that frames the experience and ourselves negatively and this can cause us to disconnect and drive away contact in a vicious circle. Escaping from loneliness requires that we engage with at least one other person and this vicious circle can make us turn away from this.

The trick here is to use any feelings of loneliness as a trigger to remind us to reach out and connect.

Isolation is not necessarily a problem; we can be alone and happy. Introverts may enjoy a period away from the bustle of the office. Loneliness is also a subjective feeling, you can be lonely in the midst of people or content on your own, so individual responses to this will differ widely.

Three factors interrelate in creating a specific individual's propensity to feel lonely

- different people have different levels of sensitivity to a lack of social connection
- some people can control their emotions around feeling isolated more successfully
- everybody sees their experience through their own perceptions – the way we think about it is important

Some people have reported feeling more connected with their managers and colleagues due to the sense of us "all being in this together". Perhaps a shared community experience of isolation will sensitize people more to what they need to do to overcome this.

It is important to have a positive mindset. People who see themselves as capable, accept the reality, take ownership and responsibility, and see this as a challenge and learning opportunity, will tend to be more resilient.

As leaders, we can help people act in these areas

- keep an eye on the level of connection with people in your team. If you notice some individuals starting to disconnect from communication, if the volume of emails and messages falls significantly, or if people stop contributing to meetings and discussions, it is worth having a conversation with them about why
- Add a discussion around how people are feeling about working remotely to your one-to-one conversations. Ask specifically how they are feeling about being more socially isolated

- If people are feeling isolated, ask them what they are doing about it. Encourage them to take personal responsibility for reaching out and connecting with others both at work and home. Discuss how you can help to create opportunities for an informal connection with you and their colleagues

Coaching questions

- How are you feeling about working remotely?
- Do you experience any feelings of loneliness or social isolation when working from home?
- How can I and your other colleagues help?
- What can you do to connect with others?

There is no doubt that the COVID-19 period has created a lot of anxiety about work, family, and society. It will exacerbate challenges for people with existing mental health problems and if you feel you are unable to cope with any of these challenges you should seek professional help.

Resilience

Resilience is the quality of being able to overcome adversity and come back stronger than ever. It is our ability to bounce back from a difficult experience or situation. Psychologists have identified some of the factors that make someone resilient. These include:

- A positive attitude
- Optimism about the future
- The ability to regulate emotions
- The ability to see failure as a form of helpful feedback

Building resilience is a different process for everyone, and what works for one person may not work for another.

Positive stress

Stress is not all bad. The right amount of stress – "eustress"- helps us to perform well and feel good about it. Negative stress– "distress" – however, can hold us back and be harmful to our health.

Today we tend not to be faced with the same sorts of life-threatening situations our ancient ancestors faced. Nevertheless, in today's world, there are still plenty of triggers that can set off our stress response. The brain responds in the same way to a real threat and an imagined one and will signal "fight or flight" in response to either.

As with building physical capability, building mental and emotional capability means going beyond our comfort zones and, crucially, combining this with renewal and recovery time.

You should find the practices we proposed around building in renewal to your working pattern useful here too.

Researchers at Harvard University describe stress as: *"The perception of a threat to our physiological or psychological wellbeing, **and the perception that there is nothing we can do about it**"*

So, one of the best things we can do is to focus on changing our perception that there is nothing we can do about it. There are some learnable relaxation techniques that can help with this, such as meditation, mindfulness, diaphragmatic breathing, exercise, relaxation or yoga, or Tai Chi.

We can also build the capability to address the things that are generating negative stress – for example, by learning to say no at work.

Coaching questions

- What causes you stress at work?
- What can you do, either to remove the sources of stress or to cope with it more effectively?

The importance of work friendships

Gallup has found that there is a concrete link between having a best friend at work and engagement. For example, women who strongly agree they have a best friend at work are more than twice as likely to be engaged (63%) compared with the women who say otherwise (29%).

Experts suggest that, while our work-based friendships are generally our most delicate ones, they are also some of the ones with the most impact on our overall happiness.

It is not about the number of connections but how meaningful they are

Work is also the place where most friendships end, usually when people change jobs.

Jeffrey Hall, a professor of communications studies at the University of Kansas (and no relation) researched how long it takes to make friendships, though not specifically in a virtual context.

He found it took about 50 hours of interaction to move from acquaintance to casual friend, about 90 hours to move from casual friend to friend.

But more relevant to our virtual context, he found that **how** people spent that time mattered. *"When you spend time joking around, having meaningful conversations, catching up with one another, all of these types of communication episodes contribute to speedier friendship development,"*

We need to find ways to connect and deepen relationships when working remotely. This is a particular challenge for people new to an organization.

Jeffrey Hall also found

- the more channels of connection we use to check in with a friend, the stronger that relationship is going to be
- a lack of social connectedness can be as damaging as smoking or obesity
- compared to face-to-face, texting and using social media, energy use during a Zoom call is higher.

Many people have reported the phenomena of "Zoom fatigue", feeling tired after a full day of video conferences.

There is no doubt that having to be present on a video call is more taxing than simply sending a text. However, we have not seen any studies comparing the level of intensity and energy of a day of Zoom calls with a day commuting into an office, having face-to-face meetings all day, and commuting home (which is a fairer comparison). I would be confident that the latter takes more energy.

Jeffrey Hall's advice for improving virtual relationships is simple

- focus on fewer, more intimate relationships, we can only maintain so many at one time

- build routine communication with these people into your schedule

- use the technologies that make you feel most connected

Remote work has changed the dynamic of our work friendships. We should be trying to keep those friendships going or even spark new ones. But as we work from home, that is easier said than done. Without the in-person interaction we are used to, some people are finding that their best work friendships are not so strong or easy to maintain as they were.

Friendships that begin outside work are often stronger and more sustainable, thanks to a foundation of common interests and deep personal knowledge. Work friendships are often more tenuous. They tend to be built on shared circumstances and casual interactions. These relationships with colleagues are usually what Ho Kwan Cheung, an assistant professor of psychology at the University of Albany in New York, calls "friendships of convenience" – the person you talk to when you take a coffee break or go for lunch.

Work friendships die pretty quickly with a lack of shared experiences. Unless you work to create a new pattern and way of being together. Even six months in (to the lockdown) a lot of people feel like the shift to remote work is temporary, so we are not treating it with intention. I think a lot of people's brains have not made that adjustment of, OK, I have to be intentional if I want this friendship to continue.

Coaching questions

- Have any of your work friendships declined since you spent more time working remotely?

- Is that OK?

- What do you need to do to reinforce those relationships?

Chapter 6. Virtualize your socializing

"We are still human beings who need each other," We are going to use technology to recreate the things that we need." **Jeffrey Hall**

In our web seminars around building and maintaining virtual communities, we ask people to estimate how much time they spend socializing in a typical visit to the office. Most initially think they spent very little time on this, but then we get them to mentally walk through a typical day.

- When you arrive, do you get straight down to work or do you catch up with your nearby colleagues on what happened last night, what was on the TV, or the performance of your sports team?

- When you go to that first meeting (or indeed your fifth meeting of the day) do you sit in silence until you start the agenda on time, or is there a period where people are sharing information about who is doing what and catching up?

- What do you do during your couple of coffee breaks in the morning?

- What do you talk about over lunch?

- Do any of the people you get on well with drop by your desk to see what you are up to?

- Before you leave do you ask people what they are doing in the evening and share your plans?

You will probably do some socializing at all these times, and probably others we have not mentioned.

Our participants regularly tell us that if they add up the total time they spend connecting socially with their colleagues, it could be 20% of their day.

Why would we make such a significant investment of our time in maintaining these relationships? Partly it may be a displacement activity stopping us from getting down to work which is less interesting. But we also know that maintaining relationships helps us be effective at work and that social connection is an important part of our overall wellbeing.

For most people working from home, it would be unimaginable to spend an hour a day socializing with their virtual colleagues and that is not what we are recommending.

However, we do think it is worthwhile to think about whether you are getting enough social connection from your work relationships and thinking through how you can "virtualize your socializing".

At Global Integration, for over 25 years the only time when everyone gets together is at our global team meetings twice a year. Because we work virtually for the rest of the time, we know that people have a lot of catching up to do. We deliberately allow more time on day one to get started as we know people have got six months of mucking about to get out of their system before they can concentrate. We do a lot of work in sub-teams, so the content is more relevant, but every evening we all get together for dinner and socializing. We also have a dedicated "community day" at each meeting with no business agenda where we do nothing but reconnect and have fun together.

We know that we can do almost every part of our work activity virtually, so we invest our face-to-face time on things that are harder to do remotely – specifically building community.

Coaching questions

- How do you normally socialize at work in the office?
- How can you do the next best thing remotely?

How do you socialize in an office?	How can you do the next best thing virtually?
Coffee Break	Schedule a virtual coffee
Lunch	Go for a walk and call a collage
First 5 minutes of a meeting catch up	Add this to your virtual meetings agendas
Sharing a joke or experience	Set up a social channel in MS Teams, Yammer, or Slack
Asking a quick question	Use Instant Messenger

The concept of virtual coffee has been part of our training for a long time and became widespread in many organizations during the lockdowns.

It is as simple as booking a time to have a coffee with a colleague, take a 10-15-minute break together, and have a chat.

It is a nice way to connect as human beings and feels much more relaxing than a formal meeting. If you are a manager, it gives you an opportunity to connect without wanting anything. You get some insights into people's home locations. You get advance warning of problems and can stay in touch without micromanaging. You nearly always find out something interesting that you probably would not have known if you had not connected.

Instead of having your virtual coffee through a video call, it can be a nice change to switch states and have a phone call with a colleague whilst on a walk outside to get some fresh air.

It is a good example of choosing a common context for socializing and adapting it to the virtual world.

One of our clients has introduced a random element where you can sign up online for virtual coffees, and the system pairs you with a random colleague, it is a good way to build your network.

Part III – Collaborating with others virtually

We have seen that performing individual tasks when working from home can make us more productive. However, once we need to collaborate with others, we either need to travel to an office or improve our virtual collaboration skills.

Many people experienced an increase in the number of virtual meetings during the lockdown period and were unhappy with the level of engagement in these meetings. We need to learn the skills to get things done and maintain participation and engagement in our online meetings.

As we increasingly collaborate with others in more than one team, we need to understand the additional challenges this brings and how to switch effectively from one team and app to another. We also need to clarify expectations and priorities across these multiple teams and with remote colleagues.

In this part of the book, we will focus on

- reducing the number and improving the quality of our online meetings, including looking our best when working through video
- collaborating with others to keep learning
- staying effective when working on and switching between multiple teams and apps
- managing expectations and aligning with others
- working in hybrid teams

Chapter 7. Attend fewer, better meetings

I thought meetings were bad before. Since we have all been working from home my days are full of back-to-back virtual meetings. So much of it is irrelevant and unnecessary but it is hard to say no. **HR Director, Packaged Goods, UAE**

Anyone who has read any of our other books will know we are not great fans of meetings. Meetings are essential to collaboration, but too many of them are unnecessary, poorly run and lack engagement.

When we are working remotely, virtual meetings are the main way in which collaboration happens. If our virtual meetings are poor our collaboration is poor. If we fix our virtual meetings, we go a long way towards improving our collaboration culture.

In our book **Kill Bad Meetings,** we introduced a systematic process for cutting down the number of meetings you attend and improving the quality of those that remain. Before COVID-19 people told us, they spent an average of two days a week in meetings, and 50% of the content was irrelevant. This adds up to a day a week of entirely unnecessary work for the average managerial or professional person.

From our work with clients implementing the Kill Bad Meetings process there is an entirely realistic 10% or more productivity improvement possible if we cut out unnecessary meetings. This is probably the biggest potential productivity gain of any people management technique.

A study "Collaborating during coronavirus: the impact of COVID-19 on the nature of work", from the US National Bureau of Economic

Research is a major study based around meeting and email metadata from over 3 million users from over 21,000 organizations around the world.

The study compared the eight weeks before lockdowns in various cities with the eight weeks immediately following, so it may be that these trends have developed further or changed since then.

They found that compared to pre-pandemic levels:

- the number of meetings per person had increased by 12.9%
- the number of attendees per meeting had increased by 13.5%
- the average length of meetings had reduced by 20.1%
- overall time in meetings had reduced by 11.5%, Saving 18 minutes per day on average

There was also a change in email usage, with emails typically being sent to slightly more people, but these changes were not as significant

In our experience working with thousands of participants around the world over this period, most of this is not a surprise. Many tell us they experienced an increase in the number of meetings, though this study suggests this was more than offset by the reduction in the average length of the meetings. It also reinforces our long-term findings that meetings typically take around 2 days per week of people's time.

Virtual meetings will tend to be shorter as they have less opportunity for social interaction and attention.

The ability of people to run and attend interactive and engaging online meetings will be an ongoing requirement as our ways of working evolve to include higher levels of remote and home-based working. If an activity takes up 40% of our time, then we need the skills to do this properly.

Our participants tell us their diaries are full of meetings from morning to night, and they are bouncing from one to another with little time to do anything else in between.

They have found that items that would have been dealt with by someone dropping around your desk for a 5-minute conversation are now being handled by booking a 30-minute meeting.

They also feel that the rapid move to virtual meetings has meant that many meetings are less planned and much less interactive.

It is too early to say how this will settle down in sustained remote and hybrid working, but we are sure meetings will continue to be a significant challenge.

In this book, we will focus on what is different about virtual meetings as that is what is new to most people and brings some specific challenges.

However, the key lessons from Kill Bad Meetings are still relevant so we will repeat some core messages briefly here. If you want more, please buy the book.

Quick summary of Kill Bad Meetings

Here is a summary of the key principles in cutting down the number of meetings you attend. This represents the messages from the first half of the book. The second half of the book focuses on improving the meetings that remain, and we will pick up some of the principles that apply to virtual meetings later.

Say no to more meetings

First, recognize which meetings are a good use of your time and which are not.

Good meetings are ones where you need to share expertise and the topics really require synchronous collaboration, that is where people need to be available at the same time if not the same place. Meetings are also important if you are dealing with issues around conflict or where you need to build relationships

On the other hand, if there is no clear outcome, the topics are not relevant, you have no real role except to listen, or the outcome could be delivered without a meeting, then you may want to push back at the meeting invitation.

If you automatically accept meeting invitations, particularly those without an agenda, you are basically saying that anything the other person wants to talk about is a better use of your time than anything you could think of.

Three good reasons to accept a meeting invite

- Your expertise needs to be shared with the group to make a decision or conclude some collaborative work
- The topic requires live "synchronous" (same time) interaction between yourself and others to succeed
- You need to build relationships or deal with sensitive issues such as negotiation or conflict resolution with others

---

> **Six great reasons to say no**
>
> - There is no clear outcome from the meeting or topic specified in advance
> - The wrong people are attending
> - The meeting will discuss matters of low relevance to you
> - You have no role except to listen
> - The meeting objectives would be better delivered in one-to-one discussions or in smaller sub-teams
> - You could meet the objective of the meeting through email

It can be challenging to say no to meeting Invitations, particularly to your boss. We need some strategies for dealing with this.

Our suggestion is that you just ask some simple questions. What is the agenda? What does the meeting organizer need from you specifically at the meeting so you can prepare? Is there another way you could meet their needs rather than attending the meeting?

Alternatively, you can make the implications of attending more explicit – what will you need to de-prioritize to attend?

We have found that almost any barrier, challenge or question you put in the way of automatic acceptance will at least drive a conversation about whether you need to attend. Sometimes it is as simple as that.

Identify the topics that do not need a meeting

Our next tip is that not everything needs a meeting or collective work. A simple way to identify this is to use this meetings check sheet.

For your next meeting, write the topics down the left-hand side and the names of the attendees along the top. Then, when anyone speaks, simply make a check mark in the relevant box.

Topics	Boss	TL	JM	SS	FG	BN	BK
1. Business Update	✓✓		✓				
2. Status Reports	✓✓✓✓ ✓✓	✓	✓	✓	✓	✓	
3. Marketing Update	✓✓✓	✓✓✓	✓✓✓				
4. Next Year Plan	✓✓✓✓ ✓	✓✓✓ ✓✓	✓✓✓	✓✓✓	✓✓✓✓ ✓	✓✓✓✓ ✓	
5. Budgets	✓✓✓✓ ✓			✓✓✓✓ ✓			
6. People & Talent	✓✓✓✓ ✓	✓✓✓✓ ✓	✓✓✓✓ ✓	✓✓✓✓	✓✓✓	✓✓✓✓	
7. Supply chain issues							✓

At the end of the meeting, you will have a visual record of what topics people participated in. We know that how often people talk is not the only measure of contribution, but it does give us a simple measure to drive a conversation on how to improve your meetings. At the end of the meeting, you will have a check sheet that looks something like this. The next step is to categorize the types of topics that you found. Based on observing many meetings, we found that these patterns occur regularly.

- Topics 1 and 5 only have one-to-one interest
- Topic 2 is a broadcast of information with one person presenting and others only talking to share information that is relevant to them and the topic leader. Status updates often follow this pattern

- Topic 3 is interesting, but only to half the people.

- Topics 4 and 6 are relevant to everyone

The table below then gives you some ideas on how you can deal with these issues. In summary, only the topics where everyone is engaged really require a full meeting, the one-to-one and broadcast topics rarely require a live collective meeting, they can usually be handled through other technologies such as sending an email, video, or shared document.

Pattern	Diagnosis	Action
Only 2 individuals engaged	One to one – star group topic	Take outside the meeting
One person talks, little interaction from others	Broadcast – star group	Send information outside the meeting
A small number of people very engaged, others not	Relevant to some but not all – spaghetti sub-team	Hold sub-meetings with only the relevant people, let others leave
Everyone engaged	Spaghetti topics	Check these really need a live meeting then use these as your core agenda

If you have people who do not contribute to your virtual meeting, that might be OK for them, but it is not adding value to anyone else on the call. Often these are people who only need to be informed about any key decisions that happened in the meeting, rather than people who really need to be there.

Talk to your unnecessary participants

If you look at the check sheet above, you will find that one participant, BK, only spoke once in the whole meeting.

It is common in our analysis of meetings to find 10 to 15% of people in the meeting who do not even need to be there. Having this record of contribution allows you to have conversations with people who do not contribute very much.

It may be that these people are necessary, and there are things you can do to make them feel more included and make it easier for them to participate.

Quite often, when we do this, the individuals who did not have much to say realized that they were not really needed in the meeting but had found it hard to escape. This gives them the opportunity to suggest their time might be used more effectively elsewhere.

We have also experienced an increase in "presenteeism" within virtual meetings. It may be that people are attending your meetings because they want to be visible to others in the organization as they have less options for visibility in a virtual environment. If you are a manager, this may help stimulate a conversation about other visibility opportunities rather than simply attending unnecessary meetings.

Smaller meetings are generally better meetings, so taking out unnecessary participants is a good step.

Save a day a week

Take this opportunity to cut down the number of virtual meetings you attend. This will improve your meetings, save you time and improve your collaboration. We have found these practical tips can save you up to a day a week, so it is worth putting in some effort and stimulating discussions around these ideas in your meetings.

There are lots more tips about applying these principles systematically in Kill Bad Meetings.

Coaching questions

- How much time do you spend in meetings? How much of it is relevant?
- How can you say no to more meeting invitations?
- How can you identify and push back against unnecessary meetings, topics, and participants?
- What stops you from pushing back? How can you overcome these barriers?

Chapter 8. Facilitate engaging virtual meetings

When you ask someone a question after a long presentation, they usually sound surprised and ask if you could repeat the question. You just know they have not been listening at all. How much of the information do we think we have really got across? **R&D Manager, Pharmaceuticals, India**

Many people new to virtual meetings find that the level of participation is low. That is not entirely surprising as the level of participation in many face-to-face meetings is poor. If your meetings are full of presentations or information giving with little role for the audience, then moving that meeting online is just likely to bore a larger audience at a lower cost.

Online meetings put a premium on attention, and it is the participant that decides how much attention they will give.

In a face-to-face meeting we have to look interested, whether we are or not. In a virtual meeting, it is much easier to turn off the video and do something else. You are only ever one click away from your emails or social media. Presenters and facilitators will have to put in a lot more effort to create engagement and earn the attention of their audience.

We think that is a good thing.

When we design training sessions or meetings, we always think "connection before content." We want to engage with people and get them to engage with each other before we move on to the content of the meeting.

Plan for continuous distraction and reengagement

We know from data around how people interact with our own online learning that attention spans are short. Our online learning is based around three to four-minute videos, as we can see that people rarely complete longer videos.

In online meetings, attention starts to fall after around 3 to 5 minutes. Because of this, when we design our online training and meetings, we aim to give participants something to do approximately every five minutes.

The distraction and attention of participants can often feel frustrating if you are a facilitator, especially if you have put effort into designing a good meeting plan with clear outcomes. This is why effective virtual facilitation is so much about managing your own mindset.

If you go into your virtual meetings with a mindset that you will make your meeting so participative and engaging it will be difficult for attendees to be distracted, then you will not only find it easier to engage, but you will also better manage your own energy throughout your meetings.

It almost does not matter what the interaction is, an opportunity to use chat, a poll, a thumbs up or a tick in a box or the chance to be called upon by name to answer a question. Any of these are enough to stimulate reengagement and earn you a few more minutes of attention.

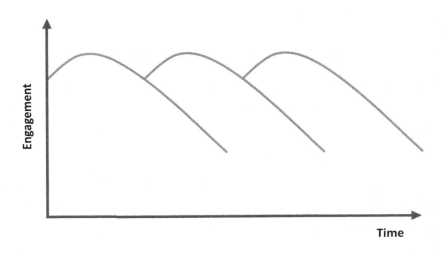

Planning for participation – OPPT

Many people have told us that, as virtual meetings are easier to organize, they tend to be less well planned.

OPPT is the facilitation process we use for designing meetings. It is outlined in more detail in our book Kill Bad Meetings – It stands for outcomes, process, participation, and time.

When planning your virtual meeting

1. Start by being clear about what **outcomes** you want from the session; an outcome is not an activity such as discussing a topic or sharing ideas. It is the specific result we want from the session, i.e., "to make a decision on what supplier to use"

2. Then define the clear set of **process** steps that lead you inevitably to the planned outcome. i.e., share the selection criteria, review the supplier bids, decide by generating agreement on pros and cons then voting

3. Then plan what **participants** will be doing at every stage. Remember – connection before content

4. Once you are clear about these steps, it should be pretty evident how long it will take **– timing**

If you can answer these four questions and make the answers clear to your attendees, you will have a well-planned meeting where people can prepare properly.

The biggest difference in virtual meetings is at Step 3. We need to actively plan a participative role for the attendees, or they will disengage.

This needs to start right at the beginning when we activate people in the first few minutes, set expectations about how we want them to participate, and break the ice on using any virtual participation tools such as chat.

We then systematically build in a variety of opportunities to interact every few minutes using the tools available in whichever online meeting platform we are using.

Our key principle is that "if there is no role for participants, then you do not need a meeting."

You are the radio show host

I have never seen chat used that way, we got far more comments, hand raises and other interaction than we ever used to. **Internal Trainer, Travel Industry, Denmark**

As a facilitator, you can think of yourself as the host on a radio chat show. Your role is to moderate the topic and to actively bring other voices into the conversation.

Online meetings give you some additional tools to help you do this. We have outlined a very simple process below using nothing but chat to create conversations. Give it a try.

1. **Start with probability questions** – for example, "On a scale of 1-10 how interactive are our virtual meetings today?".

   If you ask yes/no questions, you can only get two answers, and it can be difficult for people to say no to some questions. By asking for answers on a scale, you can capture a range of different opinions more openly.

   For example, asking "will the project be completed on time?" can only get the answer yes or no. "How confident are you on a scale of 1 to 10 that the project will be delivered on time" will generate a much bigger range of opinions. Even if the answer is 90%, you can still have a useful conversation on what you would need to do to reach 100%.

2. **Chat before discussing** – Ask people to put their answers in chat first. This enables us to quickly capture a range of different opinions. Do not get drawn into a voice conversation until people have given you their initial answer or number on the scale. Then ask people to tell you more about their comments.

3. **Ask the outliers, amplify people who think differently** – call on the people with the lowest and the highest scores or the most different opinions to explain their answers and why they think that. Be open to different ideas having value, encourage disagreement

4. **Be curious** – show a genuine interest in different answers and treat all views as equally valid. Try to use all these approaches

- o **Answer a question or respond to a comment** – if people have a question, you can respond to some of them yourself

- o **Ask the individual to say more** – if people say something interesting, ask them to say more

- o **Get into a conversation with the commenter** – get into a short conversation about interesting topics, be curious and explore different views

- o **Bring in others** – do not make it all about you, ask someone who scored very high to comment on what someone who scored very low has said, or ask a named individual what their views are about something that has just been raised

5. **Bring different voices into the conversation for variety and interest** – If you follow the steps above, you should have many voices engaged in the conversation. This stops your meetings from seeming like a monologue and adds vocal interest and variety

6. **Call on people by name** – if you ask individuals specific questions, you will normally get a response. Others will also pay more attention as they cannot be sure you will not ask them next

"Remember that a person's name is, to that person, the sweetest and most important sound in any language" **Dale Carnegie**

When you listen to professional talk show hosts, they use their voices in a very intentional way. Their intonation is much more varied, and they use emphasis and silence to break up the tone of voice and make it sound more interesting.

Listen carefully to some of your favorite TV or radio presenters and see what you can learn from their technique.

Be a facilitator more than a presenter

A presenter gives information to a group whose main role is to consume that information.

A facilitator creates connections between participants, encourages engagement, and pulls contributions from and between the group members

Tim Andrews, author of the book "Where is the spotlight" sums it up nicely as "are you a sage on the stage, or a guide on the side?"

The purpose of facilitation is to get people to engage with the subject, to discuss and create their own ideas rather than spend their time passively consuming the information we push at them.

Because it is easier to be distracted or ignore information on web seminars, we must work harder to keep people engaged and involved.

Seek equality of contribution

A large-scale study by Google has found that equality of contribution in a team is one of the key factors that correlates with team success. Teams where one or a small number of individuals dominate the contribution tend to be significantly less effective.

You can encourage this in your virtual meetings by using the virtual meetings table technique.

- Draw a table or print off your participant list
- Make a check mark against a person's name every time they speak. You can usually see who is speaking on most virtual meeting platforms by looking at the participant tab where the person who is speaking has their name highlighted.

- You will quickly see who is not engaging – bring them into the conversation

Martin	Bhavya	Christian	Miguel
✓✓✓	✓✓		✓✓✓✓✓✓
✓	✓✓✓✓✓	✓✓✓	
Inger	Saad	Clara	Enzo

Your job as a facilitator is to engage with **every participant individually as well as collectively** throughout. If there are individuals at your meeting, you think you do not need to engage, then they probably do not need to be there.

Asking individuals directly for contribution is one of, if not the most, effective way to equalize contribution in your virtual meetings. The aim is not to embarrass people if they are unwilling to contribute but keep giving opportunities to contribute using different media like chat.

It is worth setting that expectation at the beginning. Let people know that you will be calling on individuals by name at random, but that it is OK if you say "Pass" if you have not got any thoughts on the question.

A successful technique we use in our training for seeking individual contribution is the "Signpost > Question > Name" process for asking individual questions. An example of this process is: "Janet, we have not had an opportunity to hear from you today, so I am going to ask you this question. How do you effectively engage people in your virtual meetings? So, Janet, what are your thoughts?"

The important part of this process is to signpost that you will be asking a question to a specific person. It means if they are distracted, they have the opportunity to re-engage and hear the question, rather than feeling put on the spot.

You can also have an offline discussion with low contributors after the meeting to see if there is anything you or they can do to make it easier for them to participate next time.

Some individuals and cultures prefer contributing through chat, and if you keep asking them to explain their comments verbally, you will find that the number of chat comments dries up. Be aware of this and adapt to the needs of the group. Similarly, some other cultures may prefer voice over text, and we will need to allow for that. If you are not getting the contribution you expect, just keep trying new things.

Here are some things you can do to encourage equality of contribution.

1. Create opportunities to contribute in parallel – use both voice and chat so people with something to say can be heard

2. Bring less frequent contributors into the conversation by asking them questions by name. Encourage and appreciate their perspectives when they do contribute

3. If individuals dominate the conversation, thank them, summarize, and pass the conversation to someone else, call on them less as time goes on to balance contribution

4. If someone is interrupted or over-talked, make sure the conversation returns to them afterwards

5. Give credit to the original idea if it is shared again by someone else – you can see who was first with an idea in chat interactions

6. Bring different voices into the conversation for variety and interest

7. Allocate meeting roles to different individuals such as timekeeper, scribe, or process owner, so more people have an active role to play

8. Use breakout groups more. It is harder to stay silent in a group of 4 than in a group of 12

Online participation in large events

When we first started doing interactive web seminars 15 years ago, we tried very hard to keep groups small to encourage interactivity.

One of the learnings from the COVID-19 period when we needed to get training out to very large groups very quickly, was that although it did not feel particularly participative to us as trainers, we got very good feedback from participants who felt it was participative from their perspective.

We learned that it is important that participants still have an opportunity to interact and to keep bringing other people into the conversation and varying the voices.

Provided you do that every few minutes, even if that specific individual's contributions are not read out, they can see their opinions expressed in chat, and they feel it is interactive.

It is hard to process very large volumes of chat and questions in large online events, so it is useful to have a second person to moderate this. You can then pause from time to time and ask them to summarize what is happening in chat or choose a question to ask you. You could also get selected individuals to ask questions or explain their questions more fully. This makes it seem more like a conversation rather than you having to stop and read lots of text.

This can feel daunting, especially the idea of having to unmute people in large group environments. However, it has a significant and noticeable impact on the audience participation and the tone of the meeting if you avoid just one individual speaking in a monologue.

Do not give up on interaction just because you have a large group.

Create energy

One of the things that professional trainers like us sometimes struggle with in the transition to virtual delivery is that we feel we do not get so much energy back from the group.

To an extent, that is true, but the more we inject energy into the program, particularly in the early stage, the more we will get it back through comments and conversations. It is not the same, but it does not need to be projecting into a black hole.

You will find an exercise in the next chapter to experiment with how much more energy you need to put into your voice in online meetings.

Coaching questions

- How engaging are your virtual meetings today?
- How can you constantly re-engage attention during your online meetings?
- How can you create more interaction and energy between your meeting attendees and bring in more voices?
- How can you ensure equality of contribution?

Chapter 9. Look good on video

We all know the importance of making a good first impression. When I am meeting with clients for the first time by video I really must be on my game. The way you behave in those first few moments and your video background are the new elevator pitch. **VP Business Development, Advertising industry, UK**

Turn your webcam on. In a communications environment where we have a limited number of tools to engage with other people, one of the most important is video.

We agree that this is a more intensive communication experience and can be more tiring. But that is the point – video is much more like a face-to-face conversation where we need to invest more time and attention, and we get a much richer blend of nonverbal cues.

We do not need video for every communication event, but when we are in live synchronous collaboration with our colleagues, it is one of the most useful things we can do to build trust, create engagement, and improve collaboration.

Using video helps us

- build trust and rapport – human beings evolved to build relationships with faces. We already have limited nonverbal cues when working remotely, without the webcam we only have voice, which is harder to engage with. Establishing rapport creates a positive relationship and makes it more likely that other people will engage with us in return

- get feedback – even with the small video image, it is possible to tell if people are disagreeing with you or if something you have said has particularly amused them. This helps make the conversation more natural

- establish presence – in the absence of visual cues, people may make judgments about your accessibility and level of interest and wonder why you are not sharing your video. Did you not get up early enough to prepare? Are you dressed?

- show engagement – without video, you can undermine your sense of presence and seem less confident. Having your video on also shows that you are engaged and committed to the topic, and allows you to signal your engagement through smiling, nodding etc., which encourages others to do the same. Being on video also encourages you to stay focused and avoid multitasking

- be memorable – as part of managing your visibility when working remotely you need to work harder to be remembered. The brain remembers things much more accurately if it has both visual and audio cues. Audio alone is much more forgettable

It is hard to imagine any role where these are not important. In client facing roles such as sales and customer service, being able to establish rapport, relationships and engagement remotely are now the difference between success and failure.

As we deliver web seminars to participants from all around the world, we know that there are areas where low bandwidth makes using video difficult or impossible and that some people are not calling from environments they feel comfortable sharing.

We need to work around this and do the best we can. For example, if you are working with your colleagues and bandwidth is a problem, maybe just have the webcam on for the first few minutes while you reconnect, then turn it off. Alternatively, just ask people to switch on their webcam when they are asking or answering a question.

We also have some European clients who have challenges with codetermination and their works councils. Some, though not all, works councils are concerned that having video turned on constitutes "work monitoring" and allows managers to check up on their people.

We feel that, on balance, the use of video is a net benefit to individuals, helping them to feel engaged and connected to their colleagues, and should be encouraged.

Looking your best on video

Some people are reluctant to use video because they do not think it shows them at their best. You may have seen poor use of video where people have undermined your confidence in them by the way they appeared or behaved.

Here are some tips to help you improve. The ideas come from our online training program "Making your best impression on video".

To begin with, record a one- or two-minute video of yourself on your phone or webcam to establish a baseline and see how you currently appear on the screen.

We all know the importance of a good first impression, so the video should show how you introduce yourself and your organization or team in an online business meeting.

When you play it back, please do so on the biggest screen you can. You may normally appear in online meetings on a smaller screen, but the bigger screen will make any areas for improvement more visible and help you improve your skills.

Once you have made your video, watch it back 4 times focusing on different elements each time and write down your impressions.

1. watch the video and make a note of your **initial impressions**

   - What did you notice that was good and what could be improved?
   - Does your appearance on video match the impression you want to create?

2. Watch it again, focusing this time on **how you look**. Turn down the sound and play the video

   - Is the webcam angle OK (too high, too low, just right)
   - Does your background give the impression you would like it to?
   - How is the lighting, are there any shadows or bright spots that distract the viewer?
   - How is your framing on the screen? Does it focus on your head and shoulders or more? Do you fill the screen or appear too small?
   - How do your dress, hair, and any accessories look?

3. Watch it again, focusing on **how you sound**. Turn the sound back up but look away from the screen.

   - How would you describe your tone of voice and vocal energy?
   - Are your sentences and words clear?
   - Do you have any distracting verbal mannerisms (erm, actually, really)?

4. For the final watch, concentrate on **how you behave**. With sound and visuals on, focus on your body language

- How is your eye contact? Do you look straight at the camera or elsewhere?
- What were your facial expressions, and did they give the impression you wanted them to?
- How is your posture on screen? How are you sitting?
- What impression does your body language give? (energy, movement, and gestures)

When you have completed this self-evaluation, you will have a checklist of areas where you would like to improve.

Here are a few tips. Once you have worked on these, you can record another video and see how you have progressed.

Improving how you look on screen

Look at your evaluation, where specifically do you want to improve the way you look on the screen?

Here are some principles that should help

1. **Webcam position** – you want the camera to be at the same level as your eyes and square to your face. This is important to maintain eye contact. Sit about an arm's-length away from the camera.

2. **Background** – Particularly if you are working from home, your background gives an insight into your lifestyle and character. Does it give the impression that you want it to on your screen? Are there things in your background that are distracting and take

attention away from your face? Does it give the impression of being organized?

If your background does not look the way you want it to, many online meeting platforms give you the option of using a virtual background or of blurring your background. A quick online search on backgrounds for your preferred tool will quickly show you how to do this. If you are using your live background, then try to sit at least an arm's-length away from that background so the focus is on your face rather than trying to read the titles of the books on your shelf and to give a sense of perspective and depth.

3. **Lighting** – are there distracting shadows or bright spots on your video? The best lighting is when you can face a natural light source such as a window and have the light falling directly on your face. If this is not possible, then a lamp standing behind your camera and shining on your face can help. A light source bouncing off a nearby wall can give a gentler light. You can experiment with the different light sources you have available to find the best option. The principle is that your face should be evenly lit without distracting shadows.

4. **Framing** – how much of yourself do you want to appear in the video? Generally, in an online meeting, you should be showing from around the middle of your upper body and allowing about a hand's width of space above your head so it is not cropped off the top of the screen. You want to appear reasonably large on screen rather than just appearing in one corner.

5. **Dress** – how do your dress, hair, and any accessories you use appear on video? Does it match the impression you want to give?

   In general, on video, solid colors work better than patterns, such as checks that can blur or be distracting on camera. Black and white are best avoided as they can be too intense. Solid jewel tone colors work best. If you want to take it to the next level, look at how news readers dress for some ideas.

   Large pieces of jewelry can be unnecessarily distracting, so think about what accessories you use on screen.

   And finally, because we normally only see the head and shoulders in online meetings, messy hair can be distracting – unless that is part of your personal brand!

Improving how you sound

This is about your tone, energy, clarity, and verbal distractions.

Look back at the evaluation you did of your video at the beginning of this section. Where do you want to improve in this area?

Here are some common improvement areas

1. **Tone of voice** – Was your voice interesting to listen to or a bit monotonous? Did your tone of voice match your message?

   There are cultural differences in how much we use our tone of voice. However, it is usually easier to listen to someone whose voice is a bit more varied and higher in energy.

   Obviously, you can go too far, but in general, we need to up our energy levels and our intonation when we are working through video. Allow your voice to rise and fall naturally and put more emphasis on key words and spaces to sound more interesting.

2. **Vocal Energy** – Video does tend to make us sound less energetic than we imagine. Here is a useful exercise for testing this out.

   Choose a short paragraph of this book and make a video of you reading the text

   - First, read and record it as you normally would
   - Second – read it with about 10% more energy and intonation than you usually do
   - Finally – try it with about 30% more energy

   Although the last one may sound a bit strange to you when you read it, when you play it back, do not be surprised to find that somewhere between that 10 to 30% more energy in your voice is the right level to aim at to sound more interesting and engaging on video

3. **Match your tone to the message** – It is important to match your tone and energy levels to the topic, there is nothing worse than someone saying they are excited about something in a very dull way. Your voice should match your message

4. **Warm up your voice** – for important calls, you might want to warm up your voice in advance, so you start off strong

5. **Be clear** – are your sentences and words clear? Try to break your speaking down into shorter sentences. Allow pauses at the end which are a little longer than you are used to. This helps people catch up and understand what you are saying. This is particularly important where your audience are using English as a second language

Make sure you complete your thoughts fully. Try not to connect ideas together into long sentences using words like and, so, and but

6. **Avoid verbal distractions** – many people have the habit of breaking up sentences with words like – err, actually, really, or like. These quickly become distracting and make you sound as though you have not thought things through clearly.

   People may interpret this as a lack of confidence or a lack of familiarization with your topic. Neither of these is a good thing in managing your video presence

These verbal habits are hard to change. The only answer is practice and feedback. You might want to have a go at recording your initial video again using these tips. Focus on improving your tone, vocal energy, clarity of expression, and avoiding verbal distractions. The principles are simple but changing this does take practice.

Improving how you behave on screen

I find it difficult to keep looking into the camera, there are lots of things on screen that can catch your attention. Finally, I stuck a photograph of my grandson behind the camera. Now I am more likely to look up and when I do I smile. **SVP, Semiconductors USA**

The final set of tips is about how you behave on video – your eye contact, facial expressions, posture, and body language.

Where do you want to improve in this area?

Here are some tips on the most common challenges in this area

1. **Eye contact** is incredibly important. Video gives you the opportunity to make direct one-to-one eye contact with everyone at the same time, even for large groups.

The problem is that our eyes can wander. We can easily be distracted by other elements on the screen.

The answer is to stare directly into the camera, wherever it is located, and try to ignore the other distractions. This is a difficult skill to learn, and you will need to practice to get it right.

If you do need to look away from the camera for some reason, to check some notes or the chat function, then pause as you do so. It will make you seem less distracted and more deliberate about looking away briefly. You can also explain openly what you are doing so it does not seem as though you have lost interest.

2. **Smile and look interested** – in the research on building rapport, a positive attitude, and showing interest in the other are critical to establishing a successful relationship. Make sure to start (and continue) with a smile on your face and look interested and attentive at what other people are saying.

3. **Body language** – In the section on how you sound on video, we talked about the importance of injecting energy into your voice. With body language, we must find the balance between being animated and being distracting.

We only have a limited area on video to transmit our body language. Our facial expressions and limited gestures are our best tools for emphasizing our message and looking visually interesting.

Again, this is a matter of practice, you might want to try turning up your facial expressions a little and see how this looks, obviously we do not want to look false, but we do want to convey feelings and animation.

Research shows that behavior such as nodding to show agreement is important in creating rapport, so do not forget to engage actively when others are talking.

4. **Posture** – how are you sitting? Sitting up straight is always a good principle, it makes you look alert and interested.

   A simple tip, if you can, is to use a fixed chair or lock your swivel chair in place so it cannot spin or lean back. This will stop you from accidentally moving around. When you move around on the screen, the effect is magnified and can be distracting, so try to sit reasonably still.

   Sit on the edge of the seat and upright to stop yourself slouching. Do not lean forward or you may loom into the screen and look intimidating. Relaxed but alert is a good look to aim for.

   If your posture looks hunched or too tight, you can do a couple of exercises to loosen up your body before an important call. Focus on rolling your shoulders and stretching your neck, and breathing if you are nervous.

5. **Gestures** – are useful for emphasis and to create a more interesting and engaging image, but we have limited space in which to do this. We are effectively operating in a box defined by the edges of the camera's field of view. Practice moving your hands around to see where the limits are you need to operate within.

   Try to make your gestures slower than usual, as fast hand movements can blur on video. Do not get your hands too close to the camera, or they will look enormous.

If you are not making a deliberate gesture, then put your hands flat on the table to prevent distracting habits such as touching your face or hands or playing with your hair.

If you apply these tips from our online video training program, we are sure you will see a big improvement.

The principles are simple but changing ingrained behavior does take practice.

Our final tip here is to leave a post-it note with the things you are trying to work on stuck to your screen to remind yourself to try out specific practices.

Coaching questions

- What are the key areas you need to work on in improving the way you look, sound, and behave on video?
- Which of the tips above will you implement to make the improvement you need?

Chapter 10. Grow your learning ecosystem

Collaborating with others also includes connecting to external and internal resources to keep up to date and to continue learning.

We are living in a period of rapid change; it has never been more important to your career and financial wellbeing to stay up to date with the developments that have an impact on your job and your industry. We cannot predict the impact of all these changes, but we do know we will all need to get better at learning and applying new ideas.

When we work from home, we can potentially get disconnected from some of our traditional sources of learning; the new ideas we bump into at the coffee machine or in the pub, our most well-informed colleagues, and our easy access to traditional training programs.

How did you normally keep up to date when working in an office?

Many organizations are responding by increasing access to online learning and web seminars, and luckily, we live in an age where information is much more accessible than ever before.

Alan was running a training program on virtual facilitation and the use of MS Teams recently when a participant asked how to set up a new channel. This was something the participant said he had been "struggling with for a while". An Internet search instantly returned 249 million relevant pages, including 37 million videos. The top three videos tell you everything you need to know within a few minutes.

There is really no excuse to continue to struggle with technical issues when we have this wealth of information instantly available. Get into the habit of searching for solutions, they are often just moments away.

When we are working from home, we need to start thinking consciously about who can provide thought leadership for us in our specific roles and how best to access this learning.

Start by being clear about the focus of your learning, what areas do you need to keep up to date on? Is it developments in your job, your industry, specific technologies, products or is it something else?

Second, who are the leading experts in this field? If you read the top articles online and search, including LinkedIn and Twitter, you can quickly identify the people who publish regularly in the area you are interested in. Follow their articles and blogs and ask to connect with them.

The benefit of this is that you connect not only to their expertise but their ability to review and filter information in their specific domain.

We consider ourselves thought leaders in remote working, matrix management, and agile and digital leadership. As a result, we try to read all the interesting articles and research on this topic, we filter out the best and share them on social media. We also blog at least once a week on themes relevant to these topics. Of course, we do this to generate interest and potential business in our areas of expertise, but for you it is a free source of curated ideas.

Because thought leaders are keen to engage with people online, they will often answer your specific questions or point you towards resources that may help.

What are the areas where I need to keep up to date	Which are the leading authors, academics, bloggers, and commentators in this field?	How can I follow them or get access to this information?

We also follow other organizations who generate ideas in our field of expertise, such as McKinsey and Boston Consulting Group. They are a valuable source of ideas and research.

If you really want to keep up to date, from time to time, it is also worth doing a systematic search in the key areas you are interested in to identify any new academic papers or other resources that have arrived online.

You can set up a Google alert so that whenever a particular search term is mentioned in new articles, you are notified at a frequency you select.

Because most people do not put effort into learning systematically, you can become a **relative expert** in almost any topic that is not highly technical in 6 months or less by outlearning your colleagues.

Even fewer people are systematic about applying the things they learn, which is a shame because all the value is in the application.

How many of the ideas you came across and thought interesting in the last 12 months have you actually applied?

Take a moment to choose one area of domain expertise where you need to keep up to date or know more about.

Spend just 30 minutes researching the topic, following the leading experts, and setting up alerts for the future.

Some of our clients have had great success in setting up "learning groups" that focus on a specific area and meet every 3-6 months to discuss any relevant updates to that area of focus. These can be great opportunities to support your learning ecosystem whilst building up a network of individuals interested in similar topic areas.

If you are struggling for ideas, why not talk to people in similar roles to you about how they keep up to date.

Coaching questions

- What are the areas you need to keep up to date in?
- How can you connect to thought leaders and sources of information to keep you up to date?
- How many of the ideas you have thought were interesting this year have you implemented?

Chapter 11. Master multiple team membership

I am part of five teams, I have two bosses and 12 major stakeholders. Each one of them thinks that I only work for them. I am learning a lot but can get stretched thinly some days. **Supply Chain Manager, Technology, Korea**

Multiple team membership is now the norm for the kind of managerial and professional people most likely to be working from home or in hybrid teams

According to a Gallup State of American Workplace report, with a sample of 195,000 people in 2017

- Only 16% of people work in a traditional single team with a single boss
- 49% work on multiple teams some days
- 18% work on multiple teams every day
- 17% not only work on multiple teams but also report to multiple bosses.

Our own findings are that, on average, our training participants are members of between three and four teams at any one time.

Multiple team membership is the new normal for many of us, and it brings with it both benefits and challenges. If you do not work on multiple teams yet, it is likely you will do in the future, so it is good to be prepared.

Benefits and challenges of multiple team working

Working on multiple teams sounds like a lot more work, and it does have its challenges. However, we often ask people in this environment if they would like to go back to working for one boss in one local team? Most of them tell us they would not, they enjoy the variety, the learning, and the chance to connect with different people.

The Gallup survey found that the more that people worked on multiple teams, the higher their engagement. It seems that the more complex our working environment, the more engaged we are – provided we have the skills to navigate this additional complexity.

Studies have shown that working on multiple teams can have many benefits, such as

- enabling the flow of knowledge and best practices between teams
- building "boundary spanning" networks across the traditional silos of geography and function
- encouraging individuals and teams to seek out more efficient work practices
- improving performance

These benefits only apply up to a point. Studies have found that the increase in productivity plateaus and then turns negative as the number of teams we are a member of increases. If we are on too many teams, then issues of clarity, competing demands, and information overload kick in.

It makes a big difference whether you are in multiple star groups or multiple spaghetti teams. The increased number of connections we need to manage in spaghetti team collaboration makes multiple teams much harder to maintain. Working in multiple star groups is far simpler.

There is no universal magical number of teams to be part of. The "right number" of teams to be part of depends on

- your incentives
- the geographic dispersion of the teams
- individual preferences (for example, extraverts and introverts may have different preferences)
- your existing networks of relationships

The variety of tasks, as well as the number of teams, can also have an impact – a large variety of tasks increases learning, up to a point, but can reduce productivity.

What we want to aim for is the sweet spot of maximum performance (and enjoyment), where we have the balance that works for us between learning and overload.

A particular challenge in multiple team working is managing the "switching costs" when moving from one team to another.

Some of these are the same costs of distraction we already identified. When we switch attention from one task to another, we tend to lose focus and take time to reconnect to our new area of work. This dip in focus reduces our performance and concentration, particularly if the teams have different ways of working and processes.

It is difficult to get your head into the work quickly when each team has different work practices and uses different apps and processes to get things done. I have to connect to and check several different sources and streams of information to get up to speed. ***IT specialist, Software development, USA***

To reduce the costs of switching between multiple teams:

- Have clear, standard ways of working across the teams– communication methods, reviews, etc.

- Adopt common technology platforms, so you use the same tools to complete your work on each team

- Spend time actively coordinating schedules and major deadlines across teams

- Be clear about your role in the teams (e.g., major contributor or peripheral consultant) and when you need and do not need to be involved – especially in meetings

- Give individuals discretion as to how they manage their time across the teams

- Recognize that only you understand your role, so you need to make priorities and conflicts explicit.

- Make sure others understand your role and goals on the team – and what you do not do

Some of these, particularly standardizing technology and ways of working are hard to do as an individual and do require organization-wide support to do properly. But do not give up, there are still things you can do within the teams you work in to help.

Two of the biggest areas of switching costs between multiple teams are adapting to different technologies and different ways of working.

The further we progress along the journey from remote to fully digital teams, the more technology becomes an integral part of how we operate in our teams.

Regardless of what apps, online meeting software, or collaboration platforms we decide to install, it is essential that we embed that technology into our team's ways of working – and ideally have consistent technology platforms across teams that many people work between.

Even if you are not in charge of what technologies are introduced, you can take the lead by showing your managers just how many different tools/ technologies different teams are using.

Ask people on your virtual meetings to list the different technologies and apps they use in their different teams (e.g., from Outlook email to MS Teams to Yammer to Slack, etc...) and lead a discussion on whether this is OK. You will see more on this in the chapter on managing app overload.

- What apps and processes do we use to get things done?
- Are these consistent with the ones used in other teams we work with and the rest of the organization?
- Could we standardize on fewer different tools?
- Have we been trained in the ones we use?

In addition, different teams can end up using different ways of working such as how feedback is given, what level of escalation is expected, how and when meetings occur, whether emails have everyone cc'd as standard or just those who absolutely need to know.

If these can be standardized, it is much quicker and smoother to switch between teams.

Bottlenecks, delays, or crunch points can occur when major meetings, deadlines, or reporting requirements for different teams fall at the same time. If we work on multiple teams, we need to plan ahead.

Produce a calendar of key events across your teams to see potential problems in advance. You can then discuss these with your managers and colleagues.

In organizations where multiple teams working is the norm, it is helpful to agree on standardized sets of apps and processes to use to get things done. It is also necessary to be more explicit about our working norms so that it is easier for people to collaborate with us.

Coaching questions

- How do you feel about working in your multiple teams?
- Do you have the right balance of variety and focus?
- If not, what do you need to do to find your multiple team sweet spot?
- How can we make it easier for others to switch in and out of working with our team?
- How can we align our schedules and calendars to make multiple teams working easier?

In other chapters, we will call out some other specific challenges for collaboration when we work in multiple teams

Chapter 12. Managing the expectations of others

I realized that when I work from home nobody really knows my priorities and preferences. I have to be much more explicit about what I will and will not do and flag up potential problems much earlier. If you wait for other people to work it out for you, you will be disappointed. **Marketing Manager, Private Banking, Switzerland**

When we work from home, it is harder for others to see how busy we are and be aware of our priorities. Because of this, we need to be more explicit in communicating what we are doing and particularly where we are making choices to prioritize one activity over another.

If we fail to communicate this, then others will judge us against what they think we should be doing. Many people in remote and hybrid teams work in multiple teams, engage with multiple stakeholders, and some have multiple bosses. In this environment, any of the individuals we collaborate with only see a small part of our total role and our total workload.

If we ask any one of them about your priorities, they will only see it from their own perspective. Only you have visibility of your total role, and only you can communicate your priorities effectively.

- Discuss your prioritization criteria – communicate your priorities and have them agreed upon collectively. Do not forget to communicate things you will not do. If you do these things, you start to get a better quality of incoming tasks

- Communicate realistic expectations and progress – by proactively identifying crunch times when multiple activities or projects have high demands, and you can better manage your time and set expectations. The earlier you say, "I have a conflict and might have trouble delivering 100%," the more leaders will trust you. One experienced team member on one of our programs told us many of his responses to team requests are simply two words: "On it." This brief response tells colleagues that he received their request, so they know he will follow up when he can provide more details

- Framing – communicate that you are prioritizing to do other important work, not to slack off

- Communicate what you plan to do this week and what you achieved last week

This is part of what we call **earning the right to be empowered**. Building the confidence of your bosses and colleagues to enable them to leave you alone to get on with your work, secure in the knowledge you are doing the right things.

Coaching questions

- How do you manage your colleagues' expectations of you?

- Where has this caused a problem in the past?

- What do you need to communicate and agree with your colleagues to manage this?

In working together remotely, it is essential that we have clear shared expectations of how we will work together.

The community level agreement

If we do not know what others expect from us, they will still measure us against the expectations in their heads, and we just will not know what these expectations are.

When we are working with different individuals from a range of different teams, national and functional cultures, these different individuals will inevitably have different expectations of how we will work together.

The technique for dealing with this is a remarkably simple one – Ask them!

The community level agreement or CLA is a tool to help you to have a structured discussion and gain clear expectations of how you plan to work together

Individual CLA

If you are working with an individual remotely, especially a new boss, you need to sit down and agree on shared expectations such as how often you will meet, what information you will supply each other with, how often and in which media you will communicate and what should we escalate, etc.

Feel free to add categories to discuss and make sure that you share expectations and then build a common agreement on each of these. This is a good topic for an occasional one-to-one discussion.

Topic	My expectations	Your expectations	What we agreed
How often will we meet?			
What reporting information do we each need?			
When should we escalate?			
What are our standards for contact and accessibility?			

Team CLA

You can do something similar as a team collectively to share your communication preferences and working patterns.

This enables you to identify any misconceptions about how you work with others and to identify any potential challenges

You can then structure a team discussion, or one-to-ones if appropriate, around the outputs.

You can also do a slightly riskier version of this to surface any problems within the team and opportunities for improvement. Here you ask every individual to give each other feedback on the one thing they would like from them to improve the functioning of the team.

If you have a generally positive team with good relationships, this will help you move it to the next level. However, be warned, if the team has problems, this will probably make these problems explicit and may generate some heated discussion and even conflict.

This may, however, be necessary for the improvement of the team.

One of the oldest team building models, the Tuckman process talks about teams going through four stages – *forming, storming, norming, and performing.* Storming is when we release our frustrations and talk about our problems, with the intention of agreeing on new norms or ways of working together. A challenge in remote teams is; when do we get to storm? For example, it is too easy to feel disappointed on a conference call but never address it – later, you hang up and complain to the people at home – and the issues never get resolved.

A lot of inexperienced managers tend to suppress storming because they think harmony is good or they fear losing control of the conflict. By doing this, they are stopping a necessary team process of discussing what is wrong and putting it right.

When you initiate an opportunity to storm, you should be aware you are doing it, and you should always be clear that the output of this must be some new norms, rules, and ways of working together that overcome the existing problems. If we do not develop new norms, then it is just conflict for its own sake and unlikely to move the team forward.

Aligning with others

When you work on a team, and particularly if you are a member of multiple teams, you need to stay aligned and make any workload issues and bottlenecks explicit, or every team thinks you only work with them.

I joined a new team recently. They had an existing calendar of project meetings in place, but unfortunately, these conflicted with the schedule of other higher priority teams I am already a part of. It was seen as a lack of commitment when I could not turn up to my first project meeting. **Project Team Member, Pharmaceuticals, France**

When you kick-off a new set of collaborative goals or join a new team, you should

- share your objectives and goals and discuss how they integrate into and support the team goals
- if others are relying on you to deliver at specific times in order to do their work, be clear about what these are
- Explain what you are working on with the other teams you are part of, and how much time you can reasonably spend with this team?
- Identify any priority or scheduling issues between your different teams

If each member on the team shares this information, you will get a good idea of commitment, time allocation, and the priorities that you may need to deal with in your multiple teams and with your colleagues on this team.

Coaching questions

- What expectations do I need to set and communicate with my colleagues to work more effectively?
- Who do I need to engage with to do this?

Chapter 13. Conquer App overload

Nearly everyone who can work remotely works through a variety of different apps and programs. Whilst these are essential to getting things done, they can also cause their own problems.

A survey by RingCentral of 2,000 knowledge workers around the world in 2017 found that in the area of communication alone (phone calls, texts, web meetings, video conferencing, and team messaging), most people are using four different apps, and 20% are using six or more apps at work.

70% of respondents said their communications volume was a challenge to getting their work done.

- 66% say they waste up to 60 minutes at work navigating between apps
- 68% toggle between different apps up to 10 times an hour.

Another study by Harmon. i.e. of 900 knowledge workers, in 2018 found

- 75% of workers have between five and nine job-related apps open at any one time
- The average number of apps used by the modern knowledge worker is 9.39

This is difficult enough when we work in one team, but it brings even more significant challenges to working in multiple teams. If different teams use different apps and processes to get things done, this can significantly increase the attention cost, time, and difficulty of switching between teams.

To find out what is going on, I need to check outlook, slack, yammer, MS Teams, and instant messaging on my phone, and all the project specific feeds in our internal project management system. It is a full-time job. **Project Manager, Aerospace, Germany**

The COVID-19 period has seen rapid experimentation in the use of different apps to get work done and to connect socially. Often this was because central IT functions did not respond fast enough to the needs. Sometimes this caused problems, such as when early Zoom meetings were found not to be sufficiently secure for corporate use.

It is not enough to give people a tool and expect that they will work out the best way of using it spontaneously. Some will find the tool suits their personal style and working preferences, few will take the time to work out it is full functionality, and fewer still will have a disciplined discussion about how to optimize the way the tool fits into the way they collaborate.

If we allow the choice and use of these tools to evolve in a large organization, we will quickly end up with a random mix of tools and practices. Within an individual team, this may be complex enough, but across the organization, it will be impossible to navigate.

Buying Yammer or Slack, for example, and leaving large groups of people to work it out will not give you an effective internal social network; it needs some navigation, architecture, and etiquette, otherwise, you will quickly have chaos.

As we start to refine our working from home practices and processes, it is worth looking at how we can streamline the number of apps we use and add some training and structure around them to make working life easier for everyone.

In Global Integration, we have chosen to standardize on MS Teams. It enables us to bring all our calls, diaries, online meetings, one-to-one conversations, instant messaging, and social channels into one platform. We have been able to turn off several other platforms so that people only need to check one source for the bulk of their communication.

On a larger scale, when we joined an internal project with one of our clients trying to improve communication, we found that across 100,000 people, there was no single communication tool except a telephone that was supported and available everywhere.

This had created information silos and whole groups of people who were excluded from, for example, video calls due to low bandwidth. Fixing the bandwidth problems in a small number of countries enabled them to turn off so many other legacy systems that they reduced the overall cost of communication.

How can you simplify the work of your team by reducing and integrating the apps you use to get things done?

The problem is rarely the technology, if anything, we have too much choice and functionality available on our phones and desktops. The bigger challenge is adapting our way of working at scale to make the best use of the opportunities that technology brings. This requires more than experimentation, fun though it is!

Another useful practice is to get trained in the technology you have already paid for. When we ask people on our training programs if they have been trained in the tools they use every day, usually, less than 10% have received any formal training.

For example, have you ever been trained to use Outlook, Excel, Word, or PowerPoint? Most people tell us they have "picked it up" and do not need training. They might be right, but are you confident you know all that these tools can do? Are you confident that you are using them in the most productive way?

When Alan started his first job, he persuaded his boss to give him extensive training in Excel and became a professional user. He was stunned to find many mistakes in some critical spreadsheets. Not only that, but many of the processes that were manual could be automated, saving hours of work that could be spent more productively. Within a few months, he was seen as the company expert in analysis and brought in by senior leaders to explain what he had learned.

In our experience, there is always a productivity gain to be had from training people in the tools they use every day. Why not give it a try?

Coaching questions

- How many apps do you need to do your work?
- Do you find it is a challenge to switch between them?
- How could we get the same functionality from a more limited number of different apps?
- Have we been trained in the tools we use every day?

Chapter 14. Succeed in Hybrid Teams

A hybrid team seems like it could give us the best of both worlds, time to focus at home and the chance to meet our colleagues in the office. I am sure it is not as simple as that, but I am optimistic. **HR Business Partner, Consumer Packaged Goods, Mexico**

Hybrid teams are not new. In many virtual teams, there is a dominant location where several people are based together, and other people collaborate as part of the team but rarely get face-to-face.

In today's hybrid teams, we may have a variety of working modes - people working full time in the office, people who attend for part of the week, and people who are permanently home based or working from other remote locations.

In many cases, it will be rare for all members of the team to be in the office at the same time. In others, team members may be in the office together 2 or 3 days per week.

People who worked mainly from home but had the opportunity to go into the office 1 or 2 days per week were the most engaged group of employees prior to COVID-19, so there are some real opportunities here. However, this form of work is new to many people, and we need to be thoughtful about how we organize our work and create a level playing field for our team members.

This chapter includes some principles for working in complex hybrid teams with mixed ways of working.

Equality of contribution

As we have seen, equality of contribution is important to team effectiveness. Teams where some individuals dominate communication or there are different levels of communication between individuals are far less effective.

In meetings where there are several people physically present in a single location, it is extremely difficult to keep the remote attendees engaged and take account of their views. People joining remotely nearly always feel excluded.

If we work in a hybrid team where all individuals can get together from time to time, then we should try to schedule our most important meetings and collaborative work to occur whilst people are face-to-face. However, this will not be possible in many distributed hybrid or fully virtual teams or for everyday meetings.

As a result, many organizations have found that meetings where all people are not at the same location should be run **virtually for everyone**. We should, therefore, normally apply good virtual team practices to our communication.

This might seem to put the people in the dominant location at a disadvantage to how things were done in the past, but the overall experience for participants as a whole is significantly better.

On a similar theme, hybrid team leaders need to pay attention to who they are spending time with. It is easy to fall into the pattern of spending more time with the people who are closer to you in an office. This sends strong signals to your team about the relative status and importance of different team members.

Other team principles

Here are some additional principles that we have found useful in working with hybrid teams.

Avoid differential treatment – when some members are permanently remote, they often feel left out when important decisions are made, or information is shared when they are not present. We need to make extra effort to communicate as equally as we can. This means, as far as possible, communicating the same message through the same media at the same time.

Be aware of proximity bias – this can mean that people value the work they can see more highly than the work they cannot or think the people they can see are working harder than the ones they cannot. This can have implications for perceptions that team members have of each other and for performance evaluation and career development.

We need leaders to be more attuned to this and to seek out objective information to balance this bias. We also need individual team members to communicate more proactively about their activities, priorities, and achievements to keep this visible to their boss and colleagues.

Avoid an "**us and them**" mindset, which can develop if the office based or the remote based people feel the other group is getting preferential treatment, such as more flexibility, perks, or better work life balance. We should make attempts to replicate these benefits in both groups where possible, for example, by giving more working flexibility to people who work from the office as well as those working from home. We need to keep this on our leadership agenda to ensure that any tensions are surfaced early and dealt with.

Cluster around shared goals – creating a small cluster of four to six people who share a common collaborative goal means they need to connect to each other regularly and are small enough to have interactive and engaging discussions. If the team is larger than this, then multiple and overlapping sub-teams can prevent the formation of cliques and keep everyone involved.

Make time for relationship and culture-building – for people who are working exclusively remotely, it is more challenging to establish and maintain relationships. For new people particularly, learning the culture of the organization and the networks they need to get things done are challenging. We need to pay more attention to onboarding. Having an experienced "buddy" is a good way to help with this.

Meet face-to-face from time to time – it is extremely useful for remote and hybrid teams to have the opportunity to meet face-to-face when they can. Many teams work perfectly well and only meet once or twice per year. When we do have these meetings, we should focus on the things that are hard to do remotely, like building trust and relationships and sharing learning, rather than sitting through lots of presentations that could have been emailed or recorded as a video.

Be explicit about working norms – Because the precise shape of hybrid teams will vary widely, we need to be more explicit about the norms of how we will work together. For example, a global team with people spread around the world in different clusters will have different needs from one that is made up of permanent office based and permanent remote people.

We need to have a process for discussing and agreeing on these norms and communicating to the people who need to know, both inside and outside the team.

Clarify interfaces with other teams – The more flexibility we offer in the hours and the way we work, the more explicit we will need to be with other teams and bodies we collaborate with.

Some hybrid teams will give employees more flexibility on the actual hours they work. This brings increased complexity in scheduling things like internal and external meetings. If your availability has consequences for other teams, you need to negotiate this with them rather than take unilateral decisions.

When we run interface workshops between teams, we find it useful to start by looking at the flow of work between the teams, how information and work are transmitted from one to the other. We then focus on critical communication methods and events. These are two good places to start in considering your interfaces.

What would a hybrid team day in the office look like?

Many hybrid teams will sometimes be able to spend some time together in the same location. For teams where people are spending, for example, three days a week working from home and two days a week in the office, we can use that office time to overcome many of the potential disadvantages of a fully virtual way of working.

Many of the virtual teams we worked with before the pandemic only met up once or twice a year.

When we can get together, what should we focus on?

- Intensive collaboration – delivering tasks that require synchronous, collective, and spaghetti collaboration. Things where we need the additional bandwidth of being face-to-face to deliver. Focus on things that would be too difficult or too slow to deliver through virtual meetings

- Building and maintaining community – having some unstructured time together to reinforce relationships and socialize
- Common learning – sharing experiences and learnings in a targeted way that are relevant to everybody
- Dealing with conflict or difficult interpersonal issues between individuals
- Discussing issues that are important to individuals such as personal development where you may prefer to get face-to-face

The flipside of this is that we should not be spending our scarce face-to-face time on

- meetings where there is no role for participants but to sit and listen
- sharing information that could be sent through technology
- doing individual work

If the focus of the time we spend in the office changes, this should have consequences for how we design and use our office spaces.

With one of our clients, we visited an advertising agency in New York City that employed an "office experience manager". They were responsible for curating all aspects of someone's visit to their office to ensure that it reinforced the company values and created a positive employee or client experience.

If you were curating the office experience for your hybrid team, what would be different than it was before? If we optimize for hybrid working.

- we will need less dedicated space for individual working, hot desking may become more common as should spaces where people can join virtual meetings without disturbing others
- we will need more social spaces to enable people to gather in unstructured ways in one-to-ones and small groups
- we will need relatively more collective working spaces

It will be interesting to see how this evolves.

When we discussed this with our own central team at Global Integration during the lockdowns, we asked them what they missed about working in the office. Overwhelmingly it was the social contact that they missed. As they already knew each other well, they felt they could maintain their community remotely but wanted to meet up once every two to four weeks to reconnect.

Looking at the economics of this, it would be cheaper for us to host a monthly get together at a nice hotel, book a meeting room and lunch, and get rid of our office.

Unlike some organizations, we are not rushing to get rid of real estate at this stage. It is worth waiting to see how patterns of work stabilize after this atypical situation. We suspect there will be a drift back towards more office working over time. The trick will be to be mindful about it and not just go back unthinkingly to an old pattern of work. For most teams, there will certainly be things we want to keep about this period of remote working, and some aspects of the old way of working that we will welcome back.

Coaching questions

- What expectations and norms do we need to have in place to succeed as a hybrid team?
- How will we schedule our collective time together?
- What will we focus on when we are together?

Part IV – Staying visible and connected when we are apart

It is both a human and a business need to stay visible to, and connected with our colleagues

When people work from home, this is normally delivered through technology. But it is not the technology that makes the difference, it is the way we structure our communication and use the tools that matters.

In this part of the book, we will outline some principles for managing these challenges

- How can we avoid "out of sight out of mind" and stay visible when working remotely?
- How can we develop and engage our network to manage our exposure and to get things done?
- How can we maintain our community by developing the right heartbeat or cadence of communication?

Chapter 15. Stay visible when working remotely

One of the consistent major concerns that people working in virtual teams have expressed to us over the last 25 years has been "how do I stay visible when working remotely".

Visibility is important to building your network and career success and for attracting support and resources for the things you are working on.

It is also about actively communicating your value and expertise to those who need it and getting access to the expertise of others.

In the training industry, we try hard to be thought leaders in remote and virtual working, matrix management, and agile and digital leadership. But how will anyone know you are a thought leader if you do not tell anyone?

It is not enough for us to know; we need to be easy to find and to share our ideas openly. A lot of our training business comes from people who first read our books, read our blogs, or watch our videos. If you like our ideas, you will probably love our training.

For obvious reasons, it is much harder to be visible when you work remotely.

In the past I could walk around the building, look through the meeting room windows, glance across the office and see people working hard. I could even drop in and join a discussion if it looked interesting. Today I do not have any of those. It is like a black box, Unless I am actually in the meeting, all the work going on is invisible to me. I trust my people, but it is very different. **MD, Telecoms, Spain**.

As we have seen, proximity bias means that we tend to ascribe more value to the things we can observe. The converse of this is that we undervalue what we do not see. This can have serious consequences for people who work remotely, particularly in their career development.

Several years ago, we came across a study in one of our clients who tried to identify the factors that went into determining how and why some individuals were perceived by their colleagues as being more effective contributors than others.

They called this study **The Perception of Individual Effectiveness,** and they found three key elements that went into determining this.

1. Performance—the results of your work, output, and achievements
2. Image – the picture of yourself that is received by others, your reputation, and what others say about you when you are not there
3. Exposure – who knows about you?

The PIE model is a commonly used model, we are not entirely sure who invented it as it has been around for a long time. It is mentioned in the book Empowering Yourself: The Organizational Game Revealed, by Harvey J Coleman, so he may be the originator.

Most of our participants can make a reasonable guess on what the three factors are. However, it becomes more controversial when we ask people how much they think the three factors each contribute to the overall perception of effectiveness.

Many people feel performance is the most important issue, and many more think it should be. The research, however, shows that this is often only about 10% of the overall perception

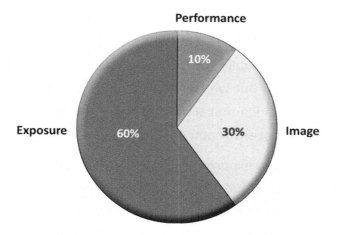

Performance

Many people in our programs, particularly the engineers, feel this is too low but fear that it is correct.

We think that performance is the "entry ticket" to the discussion. If you are not performing to an adequate level, then no one is discussing you in the context of effectiveness. If you are already performing well, then the other factors become important.

It does, however, raise an important point; we are going to assume your performance is good. If your performance is terrible, our strong advice is do not try to improve your visibility!

The second factor, our image, represents another 30% of the perception of effectiveness.

Exposure is the most important factor at 60%.

Do not get too hung up on these percentages, they are about perception and they are definitely not our advice on how you should spend your time. However, they may well reflect their relative importance in terms of how others see you. Successful people spend some of their time and energy on all these things.

Most individuals naturally focus most on performance, and that is how it should be. But we should not forget the other two. You cannot rely on the idea that simply doing a great job is enough to be visible in a virtual environment.

Managing image and exposure is about communicating your value to the organization so that others know how you can help them and how they can help you. It is not about relentless self-promotion. We are not advising you to become a corporate politician (or indeed a real politician) where style is more important than substance.

You can work on your PIE as an individual or, if you are a manager, you can work on it for your team or overall organization.

- Start by defining who you need to be visible to? Because this is largely about managing perception, it is important to understand who you are trying to be visible to perform your current role effectively and for your future career development.

- Find out what they think about you now? The only way to do this is to go and ask, so be prepared to get some feedback from your key stakeholders

- Work out what you want them to think about you? This sounds like a simple question but can take a lot of thinking about. At the level of the team, this is also a very good team meeting discussion.

- Identify the gaps and plan how to close them. If you find a gap between your answers to these two questions, then you need to work on changing the perception.

"What you do speaks so loudly that I cannot hear what you say"
Ralph Waldo Emerson

When we are working remotely, it is worth spending some time on the impression we create virtually. Our first impression could well be by email, internal social networks, voicemail messages, or LinkedIn profiles.

In my business it is important that people can connect virtually by LinkedIn and other social tools. When I am recruiting, the first thing I do is check applicants' LinkedIn profiles and see what comes up on Google search. If they do not have a profile or if it is not well done, they do not even get an interview. **VP operations, Consulting, USA**

In a remote environment, people create an image based on brief and fleeting interactions – they may only know you as the person who always dials in late to a call or from the background you display on your video calls.

In our training, we get people to split into pairs and conduct a "digital footprint" audit where we each look at each other's recent emails, social media profiles, video backgrounds, and voicemail. The pairs then report back the perceptions they have gained from looking at these things. The perception is often not the one that people hoped for.

In working from home, this can extend to your video background. What people can see when you join a call is much more a reflection of your personality than if you join from an impersonal office. What impression does your background give? What impression does it give if you do not turn on your camera?

Why not ask one of your colleagues to audit your digital footprint?

Coaching questions

- Who specifically do you need to be 'visible to' to be effective in your current role?
- Who specifically do you need to be visible to for your future career development?
- What do you want them to think about you and your team?
- What do they think about you now?
- How can you change the perception if there is a gap?
- What perceptions do you send through your social media, online, and virtual meeting activities?
- Was this what you were aiming for?

Chapter 16. Build and activate your network

Your network is an important part of managing your exposure, but it is far more than that.

When we work on multiple teams, and our teams cut across the formal organizational structure, our network is how we get things done.

In our training programs, we use a simple network mapping process to help people visualize their network.

All networks, both inside and outside work, are organized around a purpose. You may have several networks with different purposes, such as a social network or a career development network. At work, you may network with other departments, customers, suppliers, or other stakeholders.

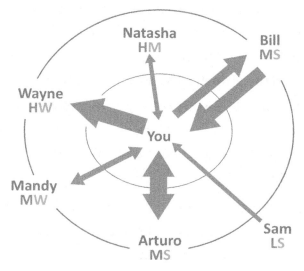

Here we will ask you to concentrate on the key network of people you use to get your most important job or project delivered at work. Being clear about the purpose of your network is essential.

When you have finished drawing your network, it will look something like this. Here are the steps

- Draw your network from your perspective, so you are in the center of the map

- Now add the names of the individuals in your network to this map. Place the ones who are physically close to you in the inner ring, and those that are further away in the outer ring. Use names rather than job titles. If you do not know names, then this is your first learning point– you need to find them

- Next, label each of the individuals on your map with how important they are to achieving your network purpose. Label the individuals with High, Medium, or Low importance

- Then add the current strength of your existing relationship with these individuals – Strong, Medium, or Weak

- The final step is to indicate the direction and quantity of information flowing between you and these individuals? The thickness of the line represents the amount of information flow, and the arrowheads show the direction

- Feel free to add any other information to your map that you think is useful. This could include what you know about how they prefer to receive information, their personality, or what they value

Our participants tell us that visualizing their networks helps them make their network relationships much clearer and that any problems tend to jump off the page

It helps to explain your map to another person. Why not ask a colleague to do this exercise and then spend some time discussing each other's network maps. The key question is, "can you achieve your goals with this network?" If not, you need to do something to strengthen your network.

When I completed my network map, I realized that I had been lying to myself. I had always seen myself as an effective networker. However, the reality was that I invested my time with stakeholders and colleagues that I liked or that were physically close, rather than with those that were strategically important. It helped me visualize where my priorities really were – **Project Manager, Manufacturing – USA**

Having a network creates the potential to engage and collaborate, but it only becomes real if we activate and engage the relationships. We may have 1,000 contacts on LinkedIn, but how many of them would respond and help you if asked?

We activate and engage our network through communication and building reciprocity – exchanging things with others for mutual benefit.

The first principle in engaging your network is to understand the stakeholders. Influence is fundamentally around information. Once we understand our stakeholder's objectives, values, and style, it makes it much easier to engage with them. We can do this either by directly asking them or by using other people in our network to seek out that information.

The second principle is for you to add value first. Give to your network relationships before you ask for anything in return. You should actively be looking for opportunities to add value, to help people in your network, to reinforce the connection, and build a sense of reciprocity. If you have helped people consistently in the past, they are much more likely to respond to you when you need them.

The next way to activate your network is through regular communication – apply the principles from the chapter on the heartbeat of communication.

Coaching questions

- Can you achieve your goals with your existing network?
- Is it complete, do you need to recruit new members in some areas?
- Where are the bottlenecks or relationships that are important but weak?
- Where are the imbalanced communication flows, is that OK?
- What is working well? How can you build on that?
- Where are you investing your time?
- What have you done for the people in your network recently?

Chapter 17. Establish a heartbeat of connection

It is hard to keep motivation at 100% all the time, everyone has their ups and downs, but we try to create specific communication events designed to help bring motivation up at specific times in our projects. **Project Manager, Pharmaceuticals, USA**

In our remote teams training programs, we have run an exercise for many years where managers and team members are separated by distance. We get teams to track their motivation over time during the exercise and have consistently seen the existence of what we call "community decay".

You can use this tool to plan the life cycle of a virtual team or activity, to prioritize your face-to-face time, and to think about maintaining connection during the life of your team.

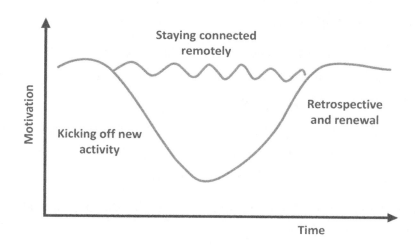

Stage 1 – Kick-off your virtual activity

At the beginning of an activity, objective cycle, or project, motivation usually starts off reasonably high. If motivation is low before you even begin, then you have a more significant morale problem.

Most of the people we meet in good companies are already motivated. What they need from their leaders is to be told what is required and then for them to get out of their way.

A well-run kick-off can accelerate the delivery of projects and activity by 20%, It does this by getting people clear and aligned and letting them start quickly in the right direction.

Leaders need to engage early. Even if we do not have the perfect picture at this early stage, people like to be involved and engaged. Managers often take too long trying to work out all the details so that they can come equipped with the perfect plan. Unfortunately, by the time they do so, the team is disengaged. People usually prefer to be engaged in working out how the activity will be delivered rather than being told how to do it by their boss.

Once we have lost motivation, it is hard to get it back. We must work hard to bring motivation back to the level we would have had for free if we had engaged earlier.

In the absence of communication, people will often speculate, complain, or even start working on what they imagine you require. All of these are a waste of time and resources.

Use this initial phase to build relationships and clarity as quickly as possible.

If you are in a hybrid team or have even just one opportunity to get face-to-face during this activity, then we suggest you do it here at the start to establish and kick-off your community.

Stage 2 – Stay connected remotely

The excitement of the kick-off has passed, and people are doing the work. The bulk of the work is being done in virtual and hybrid teams, and leaders cannot be present the whole time. This is a good thing for empowerment and autonomy.

During the remote phase of delivering the work, we need to stay connected, and we need to improve our personal effectiveness and our virtual collaboration skills. These topics are covered elsewhere in this book.

Stage 3 – Retrospective and renewal

In many organizations, we are so busy that once we finish something, we immediately bounce on to the next activity. However, there are things we can do at the end of the year, the project or the activity that can help renew and revitalize the team for the next challenge.

If you do not have a natural end to your activities, you can do this at year end.

There are at least three positives we can take from the ending of things

- recognition – it is a great time to acknowledge success and recognize individual and team contributions
- celebration – we can take the time to enjoy the things that went well and feel good about ourselves

- we can harvest the learning – run a "lessons learned" or agile retrospective session to focus on what we have learned from the previous period. We can then move on to how we can embed the learning into the way we work in the future. Even if an activity did not work, there is a lot to be learned, and we can celebrate the learning even if the output was not what we hoped.

All of these are opportunities to lift the mood and motivation of your virtual community.

You can think of your year as a series of cycles like this around particular deliverables, stage gates, or mini-kick-offs. If you run a kick-off and a retrospective at the beginning and end of each cycle, then you can be constantly stimulating the motivation of your community.

The motivation timeline

A fascinating exercise you can do to find out about the motivation of your team over time in a retrospective is to get them to produce a motivational map around the timeline of a recent activity.

Start by creating a timeline of all the major milestones or dates of the activity, the project, or the year. You can do this on flip charts if you can get face-to-face or using an app like Mural online.

The timeline is the horizontal axis. Then add motivation as the vertical axis. When people are well motivated, they would be above the timeline, and when they are feeling less motivated, they would be below the timeline

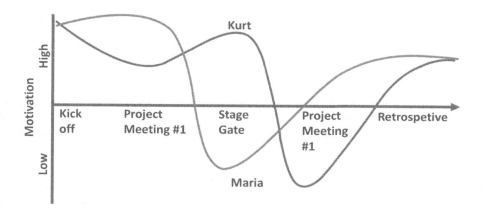

Then ask everyone to add a line that represents their motivation and how it changed over the period on the timeline.

You can then lead a discussion by asking each of them why their motivation changed during the period. You may find that specific problems or distractions caused motivation to fall. You will learn which specific things you did made motivation rise or fall.

Sometimes you will find that the same specific incident or meeting caused one person's motivation to rise and another person's motivation to fall.

My motivation was high until I got to the project meeting and I realized one of the others had not done their work. I was frustrated as I then had to wait for them to do what they had committed to. It was not until we did the motivation curves exercise that they even knew it had been a problem. Now I think they are more aware of the impact this has on their colleagues. **Project team member, Healthcare, Mexico.**

When we have done this with teams, we have always learned a lot about what helps to maintain their motivation during the life cycle of an activity.

Building a communication heartbeat in virtual teams

During the late 1970s, Thomas Allen from MIT ran a project to see how the distance between engineers' offices affected the frequency of technical communication between them.

He found a strong negative correlation between physical distance and the frequency of communication between workstations.

- Communication started to drop off quite sharply once people were separated by 10 meters or more.
- Beyond 50 meters, there was little chance of regular spontaneous communication.

More recently, Allen updated his work by looking at the impact of improvements in communication technology. He found that rather than the probability of telephone communication increasing with distance as face-to-face communication probability decays, he found a decline in the use of **all** communication media with distance.

He also found that we do not keep separate sets of people, some of whom we communicate with in one medium and some by another. In fact, the more often we see someone face-to-face, the more likely it is that we will telephone the person or communicate with them in some other medium.

For the purposes of communicating in our virtual and hybrid teams, most of us already have access to the technology we need, but we also need a plan and a structure for ensuring that people communicate frequently enough.

Successful virtual teams establish a rhythm or heartbeat of communication that holds the team together when they are working apart.

In a face-to-face team, communication is often spontaneous, and the cost of it is hidden in break times, lunch, and after work socialization.

In virtual teams, spontaneous communication is harder to achieve, and we need to make sure we have a regular pattern of communication in place.

As with an actual heartbeat, there are peaks and troughs, some large and some small. The large peaks represent intensive communication events, usually face-to-face or through interactive virtual meetings.

Because people in virtual teams are often busy, we need a framework, a base rhythm of communication that is routine, predictable, and organized in advance, so it gets in people's diaries. In addition, we also need the smaller pulses of the heartbeat to maintain individual relationships and keep in contact when we are working remotely in-between the bigger communication events.

The smaller peaks represent shorter interactions by phone, instant message, text, and other tools. The ups and downs represent the inevitable successes and challenges of working in a complex environment and delivering challenging tasks.

The heartbeat that works best for your virtual team will depend on two main factors.

- the needs of the task
- the need to build relationships within the team

Task-based communication

Task-based communication depends mainly on two factors: the pace and urgency of the task and the degree of interdependence of the work for the individuals in the team.

If the task is urgent, and there are regular deadlines and process stages, then the frequency of communication will naturally be more regular. If the task has a longer timescale, then communication may be less frequent.

Very often, the stage gates of the project or the needs of the task will define closely the need for meetings, decisions, and other forms of communication.

The level of interdependence of the work is also an important factor in virtual team communication.

- When we are working as a tightly interdependent team, we need to work together in live meetings, conference calls, and other forms of live and immediate (synchronous) communication. Spaghetti Teams require frequent, synchronous communication

- Star Groups, where people with similar skills and jobs are coordinated by a common leader, may rarely need synchronous communication. Most communication here is one-to-one and can often be done through email or shared documents asynchronously

The nature of the cooperation we need will also often define the media we use. If we are working as a group, then one-to-one communication tools will be most effective with infrequent synchronous working on the few areas of common interest. In a spaghetti team, we need to master the synchronous tools that allow multiple people to collaborate in real-time.

These two factors, the urgency of the task and the level of interdependence of the work, will give a basic rhythm to your virtual team communications heartbeat.

Relationship-based communication

But it is not all about the tasks; we also need to balance this with the need to build a relationship amongst members of our team. How much we need to do this depends on several factors such as

1. The duration of the activity – if it is a quick three-month project, we may only need relatively shallow relationships. If it is to be an on-going team, then it is worth investing in deeper relationships and a shared sense of identity

2. The level of risk or trust required – if the activity of the team is relatively routine and the consequences of failure are not high, then although trust is always helpful, it is not as critical as when the task and the consequences of success or failure are more important. The level of trust in a virtual team has been

found to correlate with retention, productivity, innovation, and a host of other positive factors. The quality and frequency of communication are an important part of making and demonstrating trust

3. The needs and preferences of the individuals in the team – Some individuals have a higher need for communication and involvement than others. It is worth having a conversation to make sure you are not over-communicating to most people to meet the needs of one individual who has a high communication need

Bandwidth of communication

Different communication media can deliver different levels of intensity, or what we call bandwidth of communication.

- Face-to-face communication tends to have the greatest weight, particularly in cultures that value relationships over the process. Because this tends to be infrequent and important in virtual teams, we need to ensure that it has a high impact

- Next are synchronous tools such as online meetings with video. Again, these are opportunities for genuine collaboration. These tools provide many opportunities for interaction with screen sharing, voting, polling, collaborative documents, etc.

- One-to-one communication, by short video call, telephone, or text, is the bedrock of daily communication, particularly in a star group. This mode of communication can be immediate, so it feels more like a conversation and is usually highly relevant to the participants. They are also easy and low cost to arrange

- Social media is a good way to stay connected with what people are doing in their outside lives as well as at work. Internal social tools make it easier to identify internal experts and decision-makers and enable the frequent but shallow connections that both build relationships over time and give people something in common to talk about when they do connect

One of the noticeable features of the global lockdown was how quickly people spontaneously found ways to connect at a community level. Within days of people moving to work from home, people spontaneously started to share pictures of pets and home office setups. They joined video competitions on Twitter to see how far they could throw rolled up paper into a wastebasket. They shared videos on YouTube of events in their local communities – from songs performed on balconies to applause for key workers. Many organizations set up internal social channels to enable people to share these kinds of events.

Some form of informal social channel should form part of your communications heartbeat.

One trap to avoid when working from home is only contacting people when you have a problem or need them to do some work. If we do this, then people learn not to look forward to our next call. We need to intersperse these work calls with calls that just keep the heartbeat of communication going and top up the tank of goodwill, those general positive feelings we have for each other as colleagues.

Make it Bursty

A 2016 study of 260 people on remote software teams spanning 50 countries by Christoph Riedl and Anita Williams Woolley found that teams were more successful when their communication frequency was more similar to the normal patterns of face-to-face conversation

They called this "bursty" communication – where ideas were shared and responded to quickly during periods of high activity and then longer periods of silence.

On the other hand, the researchers found that if there was a long lag-time between responses or they were dispersed across multiple topic threads, the quality of work suffered, and team morale went down.

The effects were strong – with one standard deviation increase in their measure of burstiness, leading to a 24% increase in team performance.

The authors believe that burstiness *"is a signal that team members attend to and align their activities with one another. During a rapid-fire burst of communication, team members can get input necessary for their work and develop ideas. Conversely, during longer periods of silence, everyone is presumably hard at work acting upon the ideas that were exchanged in the communication burst."*

Teams that do not communicate in bursts may miss out on both the energy of rapid-fire collaboration and the benefits of longer periods of focus.

So, what can you do about this with your teams?

Coaching questions

- How can you use kick-offs and retrospectives tactically during your year or project to increase motivation?

- Does your rhythm of communication allow you to deliver your tasks effectively?

- Does it meet the needs of your people?

- Look at your pattern of communication. Are you "always on" or are communications more clustered together in short periods of more intense back and forth?

- Are there enough periods of silence when people can focus?

- Do team members signal when they need a response to continue with their work? If so, do others respond fast enough?

- Are similar conversations grouped together in the same channel or thread rather than having to search multiple apps and threads to keep up to date and respond?

Part V – Leading other people remotely

Traditional management practices were often based on being physically present. Words like super**visor** and over**seer** show the importance of watching the work.

When we work remotely, this is no longer possible. We have no choice but to give people more autonomy and flexibility about how they perform the work.

This is great for individuals working from home and tends to make them more engaged.

Some managers struggle with their role in this new reality. They may try initially to re-establish control through more monitoring and checking. Most quickly realize this is counterproductive and realize they need to establish higher levels of trust and empowerment to be successful.

However, this needs to be done in a managed way. It is not about abandoning people and hoping for the best. It is about creating the right environment and leading people on a journey to higher levels of performance and autonomy.

In this part of the book, we will focus on

- Finding the right balance of trust and control in managing others remotely
- How we manage positive performance conversations and coaching with our people
- How we create an environment that enables autonomy and psychological safety

Chapter 18. Get the followers you deserve

It would be surprising if such a major change in our way of working did not have significant implications for leadership effectiveness.

One of our mantras is that **"leaders get the followers they deserve!"** For the first six months in a new job, you can blame your predecessor. After that, the behaviors of your people are your responsibility, you have either created these behaviors or enabled them to continue.

In adapting to this new reality, part of the answer lies in learning the tools and techniques that allow us to translate our leadership style to this new context. If we are unable to run an engaging virtual meeting, for example, then this will undermine our leadership effectiveness.

Other aspects of adapting are about giving up some of the traditional parts of our leadership role. This includes getting comfortable with the fact that we no longer have close control over **how** people perform their work. This is much more challenging for many leaders and for many corporate cultures where leaders are expected to have a close understanding of the detail of the work in their areas.

We see many managers new to remote working go through a period of increasing control to try to re-establish their traditional comfort zone. Whilst we understand the motivation to do this in the short term, if it continues then it can be the first step on a journey towards micromanagement.

Create the followership you need

Leadership and followership styles coexist in a complex dance, with each affecting the other. For example, if we adopt a coercive style of leadership, then followers can either become passive or resistant.

A different way of looking at leadership is to think about it from the point of view of what behaviors your leadership actions create in your followers. One of our favorite definitions of a leader is *someone who other people choose to follow*. Why would people choose to follow you?

Start by considering what type of behaviors we want people in our virtual and hybrid teams to exhibit. Then we can think about how we need to behave as leaders to elicit that behavior from them.

A few examples

- if we want people to be autonomous, we need to give them more freedom
- if we want people to be self-starters, we should not be giving them too much direction
- if we want people to take responsibility, we should be careful about interfering when they pursue their ideas

As you can see, this generates a very different list of leadership behaviors than the ones we get in our traditional "hero leader" lists where the leader is charismatic, sets direction, motivates people every day, and solves their problems.

I was a bit shocked to be honest. I always thought that by solving problems for my people I was helping them. But on reflection, maybe I was disempowering them. **Director Customer Service, Insurance, China**

- What followership behaviors do you need in your team?
- How do you need to behave to elicit these behaviors from your people?

What behaviors do you need in your people?	How will you need to behave to create this?

A successful virtual leader needs to create the environment and conditions in which people can do a lot more things for themselves.

Less personality, more action

A study of 220 US based teams by Radostina Purvanova at Duke University looked at which personality types emerged as leaders in face-to-face, virtual and hybrid groups. In face-to-face teams, people chose leaders who showed charisma, confidence, and extroversion – the traditional leadership profile.

In remote teams, they chose people who were reliable, productive, focused, and helpful. They were less swayed by personality and could more accurately assess whether leaders are actually engaging in important leadership behavior.

However, it is not enough just to perform the tasks your people need. People also choose to follow leaders based on the way they make them feel.

Coaching question

- What style of followership do you need in your team?
- How will you need to behave to create that style of followership?
- How do you want to make your people feel when working remotely?

Chapter 19. Balance trust and control

I do trust my people but working from home means you have to take it to the next level. You cannot see what they are doing, and you can feel really out of control. Particularly when your boss asks you what is happening, and you do not really know. **Quality Manager, Industrial, Germany**

One of the key management challenges in a virtual environment is finding the right balance of trust and control.

Kevan has written about this extensively in his previous books Speed Lead and Making the Matrix Work. Here we will focus on some of the key principles as they are applied to remote working.

Concern about control is one of the key reasons that some organizations were historically resistant to letting people work from home. When people work from home, we cannot see or closely supervise their work, and some managers feel uncomfortable with that. This is despite all the evidence that people who work remotely are usually more productive and engaged.

If people are going to be working from home more regularly, then those days of physical oversight are gone. People working from home will have significantly more autonomy, and the more they have, the more they will want.

An alternative is to invest in sophisticated spyware to track the number of calls your people make, monitor their keystrokes, and evaluate the length of their bathroom breaks. You may find this amusing, but there are providers out there offering this software. If you choose to go down that route, then good luck attracting and retaining talent. We are not in favor of trying to create this kind of high control environment.

The precise balance of trust and control will differ depending on factors such as the type of work you do, the maturity of your team members, and your corporate culture.

We see trust and control as two sides of the same coin. The more we try to control people, the more we undermine trust. The more we trust them, the more comfortable we are in relaxing control and giving people more autonomy.

There are powerful forces in any business environment that can undermine trust. If the economic climate is difficult, the business is missing its numbers, someone makes a mistake, or we take up a new management job, our response might be to increase control to get back into our comfort zone.

Some organizations new to remote working will be feeling this pressure as their people move to working off-site more regularly.

Of course, we need control, reliability, and consistency. But we also need trust to create an attractive working environment, improve collaboration, and encourage innovation and risk-taking.

It is much harder to relax control once you have it. It takes an effort of will to give up power and control and we only do this if we trust people and if we have a belief that empowerment will lead to better results.

Supporting the autonomy of others

I love the idea of having more autonomy, but I am not so keen when others make decisions that have an impact on me. **Autonomous Team member, Software Development, Sweden**

Everyone loves to be in control, but nobody likes to be controlled. If someone more senior than you gets involved in a decision you think you should take, it feels like an infringement of your civil liberties. However, it is easy to feel you have so much to contribute to the decision of the people who report to you.

What we have learned is that it is all about **who** has control. If you have control, we call it autonomy, and it feels good. If others have control, then it is just control and feels bad.

This flows all the way through organizations. If we talk to people on autonomous teams, they are passionate and protective about their own autonomy and freedom to take decisions in their area of responsibility. However, this does not stop them from complaining bitterly about decisions taken by other autonomous groups that have an impact on them.

If you really want autonomy for yourself, you need to support the autonomy of others just as strongly as you support your own. This means accepting that they have control in certain areas that will have an impact on you. Nobody in a complex organization works in isolation.

All organizations need control, particularly in the tough economic climate that we are all facing. Now is a good time to re-examine **where** in your organization or team control should be exercised.

In some aspects of governance, particularly in a regulated environment, you may have no choice. If this is the case, communicate this clearly to people, they will understand.

In other areas, it is a conscious decision where to exercise control. In our careers and observation of hundreds of organizations, we have generally concluded that control should be pushed as far down the organization as possible so that control is exercised as close to the action as we can.

We are not discussing whether we need control or not, we are just arguing about which megalomaniac gets to exercise it! If I have control, it feels just about right, if you have control over me, then you should have a serious think about whether you are a micromanager.

It takes a high level of self-awareness as a manager to support both your own and your people's autonomy by giving away control. The win-win is that by distributing control closer to the action, you get more and faster control, not less.

The essential precondition of control, of course, is trust. We do not empower people we do not trust.

During Kevan's period as a site production director, he experienced the transfer of control over quality from the quality control department to the production operators. The production operators were given the tools to monitor performance and the autonomy to stop the line if required. We found that control improved as it was exercised more quickly and closer to the action. The only people who were not so happy were the quality control specialists who felt they had lost control.

Coaching questions
- What is the right balance of trust and control in your team?
- Where can you give your people more autonomy?

Chapter 20. Build virtual trust

Finding the right balance starts with establishing trust. Without trust, it would be foolish to empower.

Remoteness has a big impact on how we build, maintain, and repair trust. In the past, building trust was often a free by-product of proximity. Because we were in the same location, we got to know people seamlessly over time in meetings, coffee, and lunch and at social events in the evenings.

In a fully remote environment, we can still build trust, it just takes longer, and we need to be more intentional about giving people the opportunity to demonstrate and build trust with their colleagues.

In hybrid teams, where people can still meet up regularly, we would not expect this to be a serious problem unless there are underlying trust issues that need to be dealt with.

It is easy enough to see what people do and trust them to deliver, it is much harder to understand their values and the spirit in which things were done. **IT Manager, Automotive, Italy**

The research shows that individual trust is based on two components – **capability** and **character**.

- **Capability** is about whether you are reliable. Do you have the skills, and do you deliver what you say you will?
- **Character** is about whether your behavior is predictable, consistent, open, and fair?

Do you have integrity and share our values, and do you care about others' wellbeing?

There are three key phases in managing trust, specifically in our virtual teams.

1. Trust formation
2. Maintaining trust as teams mature
3. Recovering from a trust breach

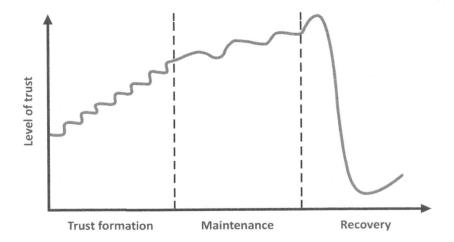

At each stage there are some practical steps we can take to accelerate the development of trust in our teams.

Phase 1: Trust Formation

When we start to work with someone new, different individuals have a different propensity to give trust. This could be based on their personality, past experiences, or even their culture. When we ask participants on our training programs how many of the people they meet they think are generally trustworthy, the answer usually ranges from 20% to 90%.

It is easy to say we should give trust to new colleagues, and this is always preferable. If we assume distrust, we are likely to start the relationship on a negative footing, and it may be hard to recover.

However, when we give trust, we do make ourselves vulnerable, and some people are reluctant to do this, so trust can start in different places for different individuals.

The early trust formation phase is critical because

- it sets the early behavioral patterns for the team
- early perceptions influence any subsequent perception of people's actions and can be hard to change
- virtual teams find it difficult to change relationship norms once there are established, so it is worth putting in the effort early

When we begin working with someone new, we are looking for evidence of their **capability** (do they deliver, are they responsive, do they do a good job) and their **character** (their style, personality, and how they respond).

As we see positive evidence that shows people's capability and character, we take a series of small steps to increase trust. For obvious reasons, we call this "building the staircase of trust".

When we work together remotely, it is relatively easy to evaluate capability, we can see if people deliver what they say they will.

To accelerate this process, we should give new colleagues relatively short-term deliverables so they can demonstrate their capability quickly, and we can celebrate and communicate their quick wins. If it is several months before people get to demonstrate a result, then it is a long time before people get evidence helping them to take that first step up in trust.

It is much more difficult to evaluate character. It is hard to really understand the intent and values behind an email, and it is harder to trust someone you have never met.

In hybrid teams, take the opportunity to get people face-to-face early in their tenure with the team to accelerate character trust building.

If you are working together completely virtually, consider appointing a respected buddy in your team to get to know them better faster on behalf of the rest of your colleagues.

A very practical and simple tip is to turn your webcam on. Research by Anthony Baker found that teams that had meetings with webcams turned on had almost no difference in levels of trust versus those that worked face-to-face. By comparison, teams only working through phone and email experienced a decrease in trust over time.

Phase 2: Maintaining trust as teams mature

As the team gets to know each other, we move into a maintenance phase. Initial goodwill gives way to a pattern of experience. The objective here is to keep trust developing over time and to deal with the inevitable small issues that arise.

Successful virtual teams have a pattern or rhythm of communication that enables the team to both deliver the task and meet the needs of the people involved. Establishing this rhythm of regular connection is essential to maintaining trust.

In virtual teams, it can be harder to notice trust problems. Trust problems usually start between a couple of individuals before they become a wider problem. Symptoms that you may have a problem may include defensiveness, withdrawing from team communications, delay in delivery, defensiveness, competition, or aggression between team members.

It is important to deal with these issues quickly with the individuals concerned before they infect the rest of the team.

Another major step you can take at this stage is to look for opportunities to give people more autonomy. Giving people more control shows that you trust people and accelerates trust for the team. If we do not relax our control from time to time as people become more capable and trustworthy, then they will eventually reach a ceiling where they feel frustrated and held back.

Phase 3: Recovering from a trust breach

Let us hope that a major trust breach never happens in your virtual team, but if it does, it can be hard to repair. If we do have a trust breach, trust tends to fall very far and very fast, often below the level it was at before we got to know someone.

Once trust is broken, we tend to forget the good aspects of the previous relationships and see everything through a lens of mistrust. With the limited bandwidth of communication we have when we work remotely, this can be really challenging to resolve.

Again, the difference between character and capability matters here.

If an individual works hard and tries their best but fails because they did not have the skills or capability, it is usually possible to forgive them. We will want to make sure that they acknowledge the mistake and receive training or other capability building first, but then we can resume building the staircase of trust.

However, if an individual shows a failure of character or integrity, this is much harder to forgive. Character is hard to change, and once you have shown you are willing to act this way, who knows if you will do it again?

Character breaches are much harder to recover from virtually. We have many opportunities to demonstrate capability and reliability, but few opportunities to convincingly demonstrate that we have changed our character.

In decades of experience with managing these kinds of issues, we are pessimistic about the likelihood of people fundamentally changing their character at work. It is important to investigate the issue to satisfy yourself that it is not just a difference in how people behave or a misunderstanding. If it is truly a character or values difference, then it might be time to talk to HR about moving the individual out of the team.

If you are new to leading remote teams, then building, maintaining, and repairing trust actively should be on your leadership agenda. Trust is harder to build and easier to lose in virtual teams, and it is essential to engagement and productivity.

Coaching questions

- How are trust levels between the individuals in your team?

- How do you bring new people into the team and establish their trustworthiness?

- How can you take the next steps towards building even more trust?

Chapter 21. Run positive remote performance conversations

There are a few things that are different about performance management in a remote setting and many underlying principles that are unchanged.

This chapter focuses on what is different in how we apply positive ongoing performance conversations in an environment where people spend at least part of their time working remotely.

Our assumption throughout is that our intent is to manage performance, develop people, and improve empowerment at the same time.

Performance management vs performance conversations

I hate appraisals, they feel so artificial, but I do like to get some one-on-one time with my manager to talk things through when I need her **Machine Learning Specialist, Financial Services, Hungary**

The purpose of traditional performance management is to connect an organization's culture, business goals, and strategy to individual performance.

Performance management is often an unpopular process with managers and individuals, and it can become bureaucratic and time consuming. Because formal appraisals are often related to pay and promotions, people try to game them and feel defensive about admitting areas that need improvement. Few managers believe they do performance management well.

On the other hand, accountability is important, performance can vary between individuals, not everyone performs well, and the world keeps on changing, so we do need to support continued performance improvements.

We need to find a way to have positive and supportive conversations about performance as well as managing the occasional need to take stronger action around sustained underperformance.

There should be 4 positive outcomes from performance conversations

1. Helping everyone know what is expected of them – clarifying and aligning future goals and priorities with business needs

2. Improving the system of work – removing barriers and improving the environment to enable performance.

3. Providing constructive feedback, processing learning, giving recognition, and holding people accountable

4. Focusing on personal development – discussing personal development, coaching around strengths, discussing careers, learning, and work opportunities.

If performance management is just an annual process that focuses on criticizing past efforts and determining pay and promotions, it tends to reduce performance, not improve it.

To improve your performance management process, ask people what they want out of the process? Performance conversations do not focus on completing a form or formal process so they can be much more tailored to the specific individual and set of circumstances.

The role of the appraisal snapshot? Some organizations are moving away from formal appraisals as they find them time consuming and ineffective in developing people.

If you have effective performance management conversations in place during the year, then you should have all the information you need to conduct an appraisal as a snapshot of the total process.

It may be necessary in your organization to feed appraisal outputs into career development plans and/or reward systems – and this is part of what makes it difficult to have an open conversation about development needs.

The secret then is to separate the conversations about the four positive outcomes above from this formal process so we can have more regular, more open conversations about them.

We will not be talking more about the formal appraisal process as, if you work in an organization that has one, you will need to follow this process. Our recommendations can fit around this.

What is different about doing it remotely

The good news about managing performance remotely is that in general people are more productive when working remotely. Before COVID-19, studies consistently showed an increase in performance in remote workers.

During the pandemic where people experienced significantly more distractions in working from home than normal, people still reported higher levels of productivity, particularly in the performance of individual tasks.

This is an important realization as managers new to remote working sometimes feel outside their comfort zone and have, usually unwarranted, concerns about the performance of their people.

Proximity bias is the, usually incorrect, assumption that people produce better work if they are physically present in the office, and managers can see and hear them doing their jobs.

So, in general, it is safe to start by assuming that working remotely is a positive development for performance.

We also advise leaders not to overestimate the value of their presence. Most people like to be left alone to do their work, provided they can contact you when they need you. Fewer than 7% of people in a remote working study felt that not having a manager present reduced their productivity.

Think about your own manager, even if they are a great person, do you want them around the whole time?

Performance discussions often focus on both what was delivered and how we did it. It is relatively easy to evaluate the **what** but the **how** is harder to see and harder for remote people to demonstrate to their boss and peers. Do not forget to find out about how people achieved the results where you can.

When conducting positive performance conversations remotely, you will probably want to have the camera turned on to show respect for these important topics.

- Communication needs to be more intentional; we cannot rely on popping into an employee's workspace for a "check-in"

- We need a regular routine – people working remotely generally feel they get less frequent feedback on all aspects of performance

- We may only see a limited part of the total performance of the individual, so we need a greater variety of inputs to truly evaluate performance. 360-degree feedback works well

- It is harder for us to evaluate whether people are working hard or following the process, all we see are the results

- It is harder to evaluate the response to feedback that has been given when people are working remotely. How did they react afterwards, and what happened to their behaviors?

- Managers may have little understanding of the working from home context that people are operating within. People may suffer from more outside work distractions

- Collaboration and the delivery of collective goals can be more challenging

- We need to establish shared expectations of working patterns, responsiveness, etc

- Social isolation can have an impact on engagement

We need to find ways to mitigate the impact of these challenges in the way we run our remote performance conversations. The rest of this chapter gives some principles, tools, and tips on this.

Goal setting – what goals work best when evaluating remote performance

Performance conversations start with collaborative goal and expectation setting that recognizes the remote context of the work.

Remote goal setting – what are you measuring

The research on goal setting shows consistently that the effectiveness of goal setting and subsequent performance is largely determined by 4 factors:

1. goal clarity and meaningful context

2. appropriate goal difficulty

3. involving employees in the process (which increases commitment and perception of fairness in goals)

4. feedback as performance occurs

Having clear and meaningful goals, particularly ones you have freely committed to, creates intrinsic motivation and meaning in our jobs. These are even more powerful long-term motivators than extrinsic motivators such as pay.

When people work remotely, some types of goals are harder to evaluate. We need to reflect this understanding in the goals and performance measures we set at the beginning of the process.

Which of these do you set goals around and measure? What do you think works best remotely?

- Inputs – we measure the time spent or other resources put into the work – i.e., hours spent working, perceived effort

- Process – we measure whether people follow the steps needed or hit time deadlines or stage gates

- Outputs – we measure what is produced, such as reports, production volumes, calls handled

- Outcomes – We measure what has changed because of the work that people did, such as customer satisfaction

- Values / principles – Some organizations try to measure the "how" of what people achieved. Did they do it in accordance with the company values or stated principles?

In general, inputs, processes, and values become more difficult to measure when working remotely. Most organizations have found that focusing attention on outputs and outcomes is more effective in improving performance in the remote context.

Do SMART goals help?

If it is already at the stage of being specific, measurable, achievable, realistic and time bounded, it is probably too late to be one of my objectives **VP Digital Transformation, Insurance Industry, Hong Kong.**

If you can set goals that are SMART – specific, measurable, achievable, realistic, and time bounded, then that makes things very clear for people.

However, SMART goals do not work as well for complex tasks that require interdependence with other people and processes, or where adapting to changing situations or developing new ideas are common. That sounds like an awful lot of the jobs that can be done remotely.

If the objectives are not as clear and measurable, then we need to think carefully about what goals we do set and measure. This is often an argument for focusing on outcomes in goal setting.

At Global Integration, we would not set a goal of implementing a new marketing automation system, writing more blogs, or spending more on AdWords for our marketing people. We would prefer them to focus on increasing the number of quality leads that are generated and closed – how they do that is then up to them. We care about the outcome, not the activity.

Annual or agile goal setting?

We learned some really important facts about optimising our supply chain early in the year which meant I needed to change my production scheduling to make smaller production runs more often. It had a significant positive effect on our overall supply chain performance, but it made my production numbers look worse. At the end of the year I was proud of the impact I had on the overall performance of the supply chain, but I was marked down on my appraisal for not hitting the cost numbers I had been set in January. I will know what to do next year. **Production manager, Packaged goods, UK**

In traditional performance management, goals are often set annually and not changed during the year. In a fast-changing environment, this may not be appropriate. If goals do not change to take account of changing business priorities, it is possible for people to be punished for doing the right thing.

On the other hand, circumstances may change so that you achieve goals without significant effort. We had set the objective in 2020 to reduce our business' carbon footprint. By March, nearly all face-to-face training around the world had been converted to virtual delivery by web seminar. We massively exceeded our goal, but it is hard to claim the credit.

More frequent goal setting can help us realign our priorities during the year, although we need to be careful that this does not become an exercise in avoiding accountability for goals that were not delivered.

In agile working, we break down goals into shorter term (usually 2-4 week) sprints with clear deliverables. At the end of each sprint, we conduct a retrospective to see what we have learned and what we have achieved. You can align these objective sprints/retrospectives around the frequency of your one-to-one conversations.

This more evolutionary method of goal setting enables us to change our performance conversations as we learn and is more consistent with an agile approach.

The power of commitment

Nobody can give you a commitment. They can ask you if you are willing to commit, but you are free to either accept the commitment or reject it. Once you have taken a commitment however you are accountable for delivering it. **HR associate, W. Gore**

Not many organizations have gone as far as W. Gore in giving individuals such control over their commitments. But having seen it in action, people are much more committed to the goals they have set for themselves.

You have 3 main options

- let the individual choose their own goals – this is appropriate for people who have a good understanding of the direction of the team and have the full capability to perform their job

- collaborative goal setting – this may be best where individuals can only perform goals as part of a team, or similar goals are required for a group of people

- goals are given by leaders – these may be most useful during a time of crisis, change, or when new information needs to be brought into the goal setting

The more the individual has control over their goals, the higher their commitment, so it is always useful to have some goals that are proposed by the individual.

What is the mixture in your team?

Setting remote working expectations

As well as setting goals, it is important that we have clear expectations about how we will work together remotely, in this case between the manager and the individual, but also between individuals who need to collaborate closely.

As part of your positive performance conversations, you should make these expectations explicit. If you do not, then you will probably be measuring each other against criteria that are in your heads but unknown to the other.

Here are some questions to get you started with an expectation setting conversation

- during what hours are each of you accessible to the other?
- what kind of response times are you able to commit to each other?
- how often and using which media will you communicate?
- what kind of issues do you expect to be informed about or have escalated?
- how do you expect people to prioritize when they face competing goals?

Clear, shared expectations will help prevent misunderstandings when working remotely and help you evolve a pattern of work that works for both of you. The Community Level Agreement tools from our chapter on managing the expectations of others can help you do this.

Coaching on improving the system of work

Few people perform in a vacuum. Most rely heavily for their success on the performance of others and on the system of work that surrounds them.

The performance of people working from home can also be impacted by their personal living circumstances, working space, and available tools. Showing an interest in these factors and helping people overcome any barriers to performance can increase engagement significantly.

Positive performance conversations should incorporate discussions around how we can make the system of work around the individual support their performance more effectively. This should involve conversations about relationships with colleagues, helping them build their network or improve relationships.

It might also include coaching about some of the issues we talk about in this book, such as establishing boundaries and a productive pattern of work.

Even the most motivated individual cannot perform to their full potential if the system around them gets in the way.

Coaching questions

- what gets in the way of your productivity at work when working remotely?

- which of our business processes and policies helps and hinders your work?
- what would make your working from home experience easier?

Holding people to account

Accountability is important, otherwise, goals become meaningless. People are more committed to and more likely to deliver goals where their accountability in doing so is clear.

If we set goals and never go back and review whether they were achieved, then people will assume that they were not important.

Unfortunately, in many organizations, accountability is associated with being to blame if something goes wrong. If we only use accountability in this negative way, then why would anyone volunteer to be accountable? In a culture where accountability is backward looking and designed to establish blame, it makes complete sense to avoid individual accountability.

The real benefit of accountability is when it is **forward-looking and positive**, getting people engaged in creating the desired result.

In our projects we define in advance a list of the people who get to celebrate when we succeed. It is a positive way of establishing accountability and stops people who had no part in our success jumping on the bandwagon afterwards if it goes well. **Project manager, Speciality materials, Germany**

As part of our ongoing positive performance conversations, we need to review whether goals were met. This also relates back to the goals we set, if people set their own goals or freely take on commitments, they are much more likely to feel accountable for the delivery.

If people achieved their goals, then this is an opportunity for recognition and celebration. These are both things that people who work remotely feel they get less of, so these conversations ensure we capture and recognize even the small successes and increase motivation to perform in the future.

If people did not achieve their goals, we can still help to make the conversation positive by coaching people to learn from their experiences. We can then change the way we work to make sure it does not happen again in the future.

If this becomes an exercise in blame or collecting evidence for future disciplinary action, then do not expect an open conversation. These types of conversations usually create an increased fear of failure, which usually makes performance worse. If this does happen, you are now operating a disciplinary process, not a positive performance conversation, get some advice from your HR team.

Encourage multiple perspectives

Even in an office environment, it is hard for a manager to see all aspects of an individual's performance. If they work in multiple teams, and from home, this makes it even harder.

It is useful to look for multiple perspectives on the performance of your people. If you have an existing formal 360-degree feedback process, this is very helpful in remote working. If not, you can set up something similar yourself by agreeing with other key stakeholders and colleagues that they will give feedback on your people.

You should agree on the list of people you will ask for feedback with the individual so that they feel it gives a balanced view of their performance.

Generally, people feel that feedback from multiple perspectives is fairer and more rounded.

Pay attention to escalation

When someone escalates something to their boss, there is usually one of three reasons

- they do not have the capability to solve it for themselves
- they do not have the confidence to solve it for themselves, even though they could
- they think (rightly or wrongly) that they need their boss to be involved because they need your support for reasons such as organizational savvy, budget approval, or the existence of some other control level

In each of these instances, escalation is a useful indicator of a potential coaching moment

- If it is a capability issue, consider what knowledge, information, or skills you need to equip them with so that next time they can solve it for themselves.

- if it is a confidence issue, you can emphasize your confidence (and expectation) that the individual can solve the issue themselves in the future, or you can coach them to find out what is holding them back

- if it is a support issue, this is an opportunity to evaluate whether you could give people more autonomy or coach people in the skills needed to feel more comfortable dealing with these challenges

In all these cases, escalation is an indication that the individual does not feel able to solve the issue for themselves. It is a good prompt to have a development conversation.

Strength based development conversations

It is tempting when we talk about development to look at skill gaps, weaknesses, and what went wrong. Whilst there is a place for this, it tends to focus on the negatives.

Positive performance conversations focus more on strengths. A strength-based conversation encourages the individual to build on the things they are good at (and usually enjoy as a result).

Where possible, we want people to spend more of their time playing to their strengths. It may even be possible to design out elements of their jobs where they are less strong or work around these.

If there are gaps to be filled or weaknesses to be worked on, we should address these only after we have acknowledged and built on the strengths. If there are several areas to be worked on, it might be useful to spread these over time rather than try to address everything at once.

Individuals will also occasionally want to talk about their personal development in terms of career progression. Different organizations have different approaches to this. In a positive performance conversation, it is good to help people think through the next step in their careers so they can develop the strengths and experiences they need to be ready when the next opportunity arises.

Reward and ranking

Many organizations have a formal process each year to rank the performance and potential of their people. Some organizations claim there is no link between performance appraisal and reward, but nobody is really fooled by that.

There are many arguments against a forced ranking of performance – where, for example, 10% of your people have got to be in the lowest category. Most organizations have moved away from this approach, but it persists in some areas. It is usually deeply unpopular.

The key principle in having positive performance conversations is to keep this part of the discussion separate from the ongoing conversations. It is very hard to have an open discussion of problems, challenges, or personal development when people are trying to give the most positive picture possible to influence their future reward.

Continuing conversations about sustainable remote performance

From their extensive database of performance management surveys, Gallup recommends focusing on three key principles that define effective coaching conversations: frequent, focused, and future oriented.

How often is regular?

Because positive performance conversations can be more personalized than annual reviews, you can set the regularity of your check-ins and one-to-ones to suit the needs of the individual. Very experienced and self-motivated people may need fewer regular conversations, newer people should receive more.

We will suggest the frequency of the different types of conversations below. Use this as a starting point, then discuss this with the individual in your team and find out what they would like.

What should a positive performance conversation cover?

As we have identified above, there are a number of different elements of an overall set of positive performance conversations

- Goal setting
- Setting remote working expectations
- Establishing the preconditions for autonomy
- Coaching for engagement – improving the system of work around the individual
- Holding people to account – reviewing progress and learning retrospectives
- Encouraging multiple perspectives on performance
- Strength based development conversations
- Reward and career

It can be hard, and time consuming, to have all these conversations at the same time. It is useful to think about the different context in which we will have these conversations and to separate the topics accordingly.

We have made some recommendations below on how to do this with a recommended frequency for having these conversations with someone who is already established in your team.

Performance improvement coaching works even better when we do it in the moment, so if there is a learning opportunity or a piece of feedback you want to give, it is best to do that at the time rather than save it up for the next scheduled call.

Context	Content	Suggested frequency for an experienced person
Establishing goals and expectation	Set goals for the next period. Clarify expectations of how we will work together	Annual, more often in periods of change
Quick check in	How is it going? In the moment coaching and support	Weekly
Regular one-to-ones	Should be driven by what the individual wants to talk about. Progress check-in, discuss engagement, and how to help with any barriers, learning from escalations. Coaching	Monthly

Context	Content	Suggested frequency for an experienced person
Personal development	Strengths based performance discussions, career aspirations, career coaching	Annual
Progress review (more formal than one-to-one)	Positive accountability, a retrospective on learning from the previous period, next steps, and any changed goals for the future	Quarterly
Reward and ranking discussion (appraisal process)	Discussion on pay and, if necessary, ranking into performance categories	As defined by your organization, usually annual

Coaching questions

- How are our goals adapted to a remote and fast-changing environment?

- How much are individuals involved and committed to their goal setting?

- Have we made expectations clear about how we will work together remotely?

- How often do we discuss the system of work that is around the individual?

- How do we hold people to account in a positive way?
- How do we get multiple inputs into performance evaluation?
- When do we focus on strengths in development discussions?
- Is the regularity of our conversations about performance and development OK?

Chapter 22. Deliver remote coaching and empowerment

There are many different approaches to coaching.

If you have seen movies about their stereotypical American football "coach" who gets right in the faces of their people, whips them up, discourages dissent, tells them how to live, and defines each play of the game – this is not what we mean.

Our definition of a coach is someone who facilitates others to work things out for themselves and helps them build confidence and commitment in implementing their own ideas. This approach is known as non-directive coaching.

It is best described in the book "Coaching for Performance" by John Whitmore. John uses the GROW model, where the coach asks open questions around four phases

- the goal of the coaching – what does the individual want out of the coaching session?
- the reality of the situation – what have they tried already, what worked, what did not?
- the options they have – what else could you try, what barriers do you see to this, how will you overcome them?
- the will – how committed are you to implementing these ideas?

The coach uses open questions that encourage the coachee to think and to work things out for themselves. It is an easy process to learn in principle, but it is extremely hard as a coach not to jump in and offer your own ideas and suggestions.

Because it is based on asking questions, it is not a technique you can use easily with someone who genuinely does not know the answer. If people are still at this stage, then focus on building their capability.

This style of coaching works best once people have an idea of what to do but for some reason are not stepping up and taking responsibility for doing it.

We recommend this style of coaching as one of the most useful elements of the leaders' toolkit.

Earning the right to be empowered

It is very common in our training programs for people to complain that their leaders do not empower them enough. Because we always try to get people to focus on what **they** can do, rather than what others should do, we often push back and ask, "what have you done to earn the right to be empowered".

People are often initially surprised by the question; it is not something that many people have considered, but it often leads to a good discussion.

Put yourself in the position of your manager. What would they like you to do to show that you are ready to have higher levels of empowerment? If you were them, would you empower you more?

The signals we send to our managers that gives them the confidence to empower can include

- how we escalate – do we come to our managers with problems or also bring potential solutions

- how we respond to change or ambiguity – do we try and work it out for ourselves and discuss our ideas with them, or do we wait to be told what to do

- how we communicate – are we proactive at staying in touch, or do they have to initiate all communication

- how we prioritize – do we keep our manager informed about any delays or prioritization issues and make suggestions about how these can be resolved

- how we prevent surprises – do we communicate problems before they cause our manager to be embarrassed

You can probably think of others from your own experience with past bosses or people who work for you. What made you feel more willing to empower some people over others?

Coaching questions

- How can you use non-directive coaching in your role?

- Think about your recent interactions with your manager. Did you leave the conversation having established the right to be empowered even more?

- What will you do differently to earn that right in the future?

- How can you help your people earn the right to be more empowered by you?

Chapter 23. Create the preconditions for autonomy

"We hire great people and then it is up to them, you either sink or swim in this business" **HR VP, Financial Services, USA**

Giving mindless autonomy or letting people "sink or swim" is not a development strategy, it is an abandonment strategy.

We want to give people autonomy, more control over their work, wherever possible. But we also need to do it in a managed way.

When people work remotely, they will naturally have and require more autonomy, and millions of people suddenly found themselves working from home in 2020 with little or no preparation. Even where we have increased autonomy as a reality, we need to check that we have put in place the preconditions to support it for the longer term.

These are the 3 essential preconditions for giving real autonomy.

- We need to **trust** that people can and will deliver in a way that meets our values

- We need people to be **aligned** to the direction and goals of the team and organization; otherwise, they may head off in the wrong direction and waste resources. This does not mean that we need to predetermine every detail, but we do need some level of alignment

- We should only give autonomy to people who have the **capability** to do the job. It would make no sense to empower people who do not have the ability to deliver the task. This could be in terms of skills, tools, or motivation.

Empowering people who do not meet these 3 tests and are incapable of delivery is unfair to them and unfair to the organization.

It also never happens that we move from no autonomy to full autonomy. We need to lead people on the journey. As leaders, we should always be looking for the opportunity to move people to the next step, even if it is just 5% more autonomy. If we keep doing this, eventually, we will have fully autonomous people.

Individuals in my team	Do I trust them?	Are they aligned?	Are they fully capable to do their job?	What is the next step towards autonomy

Coaching questions

- Where are each of the individuals in your team with respect to these three questions?
- Do they have the trust, alignment, and capability needed to operate successfully when working remotely?
- What is the next step for each individual?

Chapter 24. Creating Psychological safety

"Team members feel safe to take risks and be vulnerable in front of each other" **Google People Analytics Unit** definition of psychological safety

Psychological safety is being able to participate without fear of negative consequences to our self-image, status, or career. It is a belief that the team or meeting is safe for interpersonal risk taking where people feel accepted and respected.

This is particularly important in an environment where we need people to embrace change, try new things, and contribute openly. Trying something new includes the risk of failure, and challenging existing ideas risks upsetting the status quo.

Unless people feel supported in these behaviors, change, innovation, collaboration, and personal effectiveness will be damaged.

Psychological safety has been researched extensively since the 1960s and was recently found by Google People Analytics Unit in their data led search for the perfect team to be the number one factor in team performance.

The research shows that we can support psychological safety in two key areas

- supportive leadership and organizational behaviors – it is critical how we treat people and how we react to ideas and even mistakes. As leaders, we need to model the behaviors that make taking risks feel safe

- strong relationship networks — where people know each other well and have had positive relationships in the past, they feel safer about taking risks

Psychological safety also seems to be stronger in teams that pay attention to learning and experimentation. Perhaps because this legitimizes trying new things and learning from them as a normal part of the team activity.

An important group norm that supports psychological safety is "equality in distribution of conversational turn-taking" — meaning, everyone has equal airtime. See more about how to manage this in our virtual meetings chapters.

What is Psychological safety like in your team?

Coaching questions

- Does it feel risky to try new things or raise new ideas in our team or organization?
- What is it we do that makes it feel risky?
- How do we react to mistakes or divergent opinions?
- How could we make it feel less risky?

Chapter 25. Diversity and Inclusion in Virtual Teams and Online Meetings

Remote working gives us some opportunities to improve diversity in our teams and organizations.

When our teams are not restricted to the people who are willing and able to live within commuting distance of our office and come in every day, then we have access to a more diverse pool of people.

What is the chance that genuinely the best people in the world to work on your problem happen to be the ones living nearby?

Some people will point to the advantages of being in a hub location with a critical mass of people with similar skills, such as Silicon Valley. Whilst those advantages clearly exist, they still limit talent to the people able and willing to get a visa, uproot their families and move to the West coast of the USA. About 3 million people live in Silicon Valley, less than 0.04% of the world's population. 4.66 billion people worldwide were estimated to have access to the internet in 2020. They are now your potential global talent pool when you offer remote working.

Remote working should encourage diversity in several ways, including

- removing the barrier of distance to accessing the best global talent
- making us more connected to colleagues in different cultures

- giving us access to people who are not mobile because of family or other commitments
- it is an attractive work benefit for everyone, particularly women and younger employees
- enabling people who cannot afford to live in expensive hub locations to participate
- being more suitable for parents who want to be more flexible around childcare commitments
- enabling us to include more people who may be physically or psychologically unable to travel to or work in an office

Whilst it gives us these potential opportunities and more, remote working will not automatically bring diversity. We still need to work to create a more diverse workforce and a more inclusive environment.

Working through technology also gives us some new opportunities to break down some of the traditional boundaries to include more diverse perspectives.

Making virtual meetings more inclusive

Meetings are the key context where group collaboration happens. Managers and professionals spend an average of two days a week in meetings. As this is where collaboration happens, it is also an important place for practicing inclusivity. If we make our meetings inclusive, we make most of our collective collaboration inclusive.

Virtual meetings bring some new opportunities to change the way we involve, participate, and engage, and to break down traditional barriers to more inclusive ways of working.

How does diversity have an impact on meeting behaviors

There are many examples from research and practice where different individuals have different experiences of meetings. Here are just a few common examples.

- in neurodiversity, introverts and extroverts have different participation styles, engage differently in the discussion, need different amounts of time to process information, and have different preferences on group sizes

- different cultures have very different ideas about status and power and how it is expressed and challenged in meetings. They may prefer to participate individually or in groups. They may have different norms around the directness of communication or the use of silence. Some may feel excluded by the pace of native language speakers' contributions

- men and women may have different experiences around participation, in the regularity of interruptions, the attribution of ideas, or through experiences of positive or negative reinforcement

- people from different age cohorts may have different levels of experience and different levels of comfort with virtual meeting technologies

- people from marginalized groups may experience meetings differently due to lower levels of representation and stereotyping

- people who work remotely as part of hybrid teams where many of their colleagues are in the same location can easily be forgotten and find it hard to contribute

- following COVID-19 this may include vulnerable people who are unable to return to the workplace due to health conditions or concerns

When we take all these groups together, we can see that almost everybody has an interest in creating more inclusive meetings. Nobody benefits from a meeting where individuals cannot speak out and be heard. Inclusive meetings should be better for everyone.

We will identify the underlying challenges to inclusivity and propose some virtual meeting principles and practices that we can apply to overcome them.

The underlying issues

In creating inclusive meetings, we particularly need to manage two challenges

- power differences
- diverse participation styles and opinions

Power differences between participants

Power differences, whether through organizational seniority or through the membership of dominant groups, can inhibit participation by people with lower levels of power and suppress or influence the expression of ideas and opinions.

Meeting virtually can bring some advantages here as it tends to mask some of the explicit signals of status and power. It is a different experience meeting in the boss's office with them sitting at the head of the table with their status symbols around them, versus being in a virtual meeting where everyone has a similar sized video window.

However, power is always there in the background, and individuals and groups with greater power need to provide the space for diverse opinions to be expressed. We will show you how to do this in virtual meetings later in this chapter

Diverse participation styles and opinions

In a traditional face-to-face meeting, we have limited opportunities to participate. We catch someone's eye, raise a hand, and speak. In a more interactive face-to-face meeting, we can introduce other techniques such as using flip charts or post it notes.

In an online meeting, depending on which platform we use, we have a much wider range of alternative ways to participate. As well as voice we may have text, emojis, gifs, polls, pointers, drawing, whiteboards, apps, shared documents, and many other tools. These enable us to satisfy a wider range of participation preferences and collect diverse opinions more easily.

We can also run these in parallel, so we can get input in several ways at the same time. By combining these approaches intelligently, we can overcome some of the challenges people may feel in speaking up and use them to amplify different voices.

Here are 11 practical tips for running more inclusive virtual meetings

1. Use the webcam. The use of webcams has been found to significantly improve the building and maintenance of trust when communicating through technology. It has also been found to be less stressful than listening to voice only. On the other hand, it does transmit more visual cues about differences.

    On balance, we believe that the use of webcams is beneficial for inclusive meetings and should be encouraged.

For senior leaders and dominant groups using webcams, you might want to consider factors such as dress and the appearance of your backgrounds to minimize signals of status.

2. Have leaders talk last. When a person with power expresses an opinion early in a conversation, this creates an effect called anchoring. Further opinions will then tend to cluster around this opinion, and outlying opinions will be less likely to be expressed. If you are a senior meeting attendee – ask questions and give information but avoid giving opinions too early. Listen first.

3. Be curious – actively seek to understand where people feel differently from the group and explore their opinions. Assume that different views will enrich the debate. Ask questions like

   o what do you see/think that we do not?

   o let us explore this view?

   o what is behind that?

   o tell us more about that?

4. Chat or poll first, before you discuss. To avoid anchoring, capture people's initial opinions through chat in parallel before you discuss. Ask people to prepare their inputs but not to send them until you say so. This stops early chats from shaping or anchoring the discussion.

   Do not show the results of a poll until everyone has replied.

   A quick and fun way to identify different views on webcam is to use fist voting (0-5 vote using fingers or one hand). Ask people how committed they are to a decision (for example) on a scale of 0 to 5. Showing five fingers indicates absolute commitment. Countdown 3-2-1 and ask people to show their hands-on camera. Then discuss the views of people who scored very low or very high.

Apps such as Mentimeter or Kahoot allow us to collect opinions and can be run in parallel with your online meetings. Again, delay showing results until participants have all completed their inputs.

Once the different opinions are visible, we can make sure to discuss the full range of them.

5. Ask probability questions instead of asking binary questions with "Yes/No" answers or leading questions "We will be ready by the deadline, right?" Instead, ask "How likely are we to deliver on time – give me a percentage answer?", or "How confident are you on a scale of 1-10 that we will hit the deadline?"

Asking for a scale or a percentage answer brings more nuance and prevents yes/no answers. People may be more willing to say, "it is 60% likely" than "No, it may not happen." You can then follow up with questions to understand why people feel that way, explore different opinions and understand what would need to happen to increase their confidence

6. Amplify the outliers – All innovations come from people who think differently. Actively look for different opinions and bring them to prominence.

Once you have captured a variety of opinions, make sure you call on the people with divergent opinions first. Start with people who have answered at either extreme or whose opinions in chat seem different from the group.

You can do this by directly calling on people with divergent opinions and asking questions like "Tell me more" or "What do you see that others do not?"

However, if you always call out people with divergent opinions, some will learn not to express them. Another alternative is to choose an outlying opinion and say, "this one is interesting, let us spend some time assuming this is correct – what would it mean for us?"

If there are two distinct sets of opinions, call on the minority one to explain first, or split the group into two and ask each group to advocate for the opposite view than the one they initially expressed.

Please note this does not mean you always have to go with the outlying opinions. Just be sure to explore them before you move to a decision.

7. Resist fast consensus – when an opinion starts to form, social conformity can reduce dissent and different ideas and inhibit people from contributing with a different view.

    There is a time to search for consensus but leave this until later in the discussion once diverse views have emerged. If it happens too fast, try, "we seem to be jumping fast to this view, let's take a moment to assume the opposite".

8. Pursue equality of contribution. Use the virtual meetings table tool and the facilitation tips from our chapter on facilitating engaging virtual meetings

9. Make regular use of breakout rooms. Smaller groups enable higher levels of involvement. Aim for groups of no more than

4-6 people to create conversations where everyone can be involved

10. Rotate facilitators – Give others with different perspectives an opportunity to set and lead the agenda and understand the techniques of creating inclusion

11. Demonstrate that dissent is safe, especially if you are the most senior individual in a meeting

Show through how you receive and deal with different opinions that you value them.

Alternatively, allocate a dissenter role. For example, send 50% of your participants into a breakout room to come up with the case against the decision the group is proposing, and 50% to another breakout to argue the case for the decision. This makes dissent less personal; it is a role you have been given, rather than your own opinion.

There are many other things we can do to improve inclusivity in our organizations, but virtual meetings give us some simple new opportunities to create significant steps in this area at a low cost.

Try out some of these techniques, they should be better for everybody.

Coaching questions

- Where does working remotely give us an opportunity to increase diversity in our team?

- How can we make our virtual meetings more inclusive?

Chapter 26. Creativity and Innovation in remote and hybrid teams

How am I going to get to spark ideas off others and learn new things at the watercooler now I am working from home more often? **R&D Associate, Energy, India**

There are persistent concerns in organizations about the impact of remoteness on creativity and innovation. Many of our clients have chosen in the past to centralize their R&D functions and encourage face-to-face working because of this.

Usually, this is based on the fear that if people are not in the same location, they will miss the benefits of serendipity, the transfer of ideas and solutions that happen over the water cooler, or through chance interactions.

We are also moving into a tough economic climate where rapid innovation will be essential to survival for many organizations.

The people involved in the process of creativity and innovation remotely will be largely the same people who used to do it in offices in the past, so they will have the same capabilities. However, they may not be used to exercising these skills in a remote context.

We need a reengineered process for delivering creativity and innovation in remote and hybrid teams.

- **Creativity** is about generating new and novel ideas
- **Innovation** is about the application of ideas to create value

We are going to challenge some common myths around creativity and serendipity and propose some processes and practices that we can deliver virtually to overcome many of these concerns.

The creative process

In his book, published over fifty years ago, James Webb Young outlined the "Creative Process". It has been validated in practice and by the recent findings of neuroscience.

He saw creativity as proceeding through several steps.

1. **Focusing on a specific topic – defining the problem and gathering knowledge** — through clear problem definitions and researching both deeply into the topic and broadly around it

2. **Hard thinking about the problem** — doing your best to combine the different elements into a workable solution. Keep reading, working, and trying to make sense of the material until you are ready to give up out of sheer exhaustion, then continue a bit more

3. **Incubation** — take a break and let your unconscious mind work its magic. Young recommends doing something different that stimulates your imagination and emotions – reading, exercise, listening to music, etc. Expect this to take as long as it takes

4. **The Eureka moment** — when the idea appears as if from nowhere in the shower or wakes you up in the night

5. **Developing the idea** — expanding its possibilities, evaluating it for weaknesses, and translating it into action

As you can see, two of these steps may require collective collaboration (though not necessarily).

- at step 1, for many instances of creativity in organizations, we need agreement on the problem, and collaboration might help us access broader research

- at step 5, we need collaboration to develop our ideas and prepare them for implementation

The other three steps are **inherently individual** and can probably be done better remotely or at home where distractions are fewer.

We reached a similar conclusion on brainstorming. The brainstorming meeting is based on a popular, but incorrect, assumption that groups generate more ideas than the sum of the individuals on their own.

In fact, it has been clear from research for many years that the opposite is true. Individuals working alone generate many more ideas than the same individuals working collectively. In a group, people tend to moderate their ideas and are influenced by the status and feedback of other group members. Ideas are more likely to be inhibited than encouraged by collective brainstorming.

If you want pure creativity and idea generation, it is better to let individuals prepare and work alone.

Where a group does add value is in the development and evaluation of ideas. There is value in doing this part collectively – just not the original idea generation part.

Advantages of remote working for creativity

There are some very tangible advantages to running our creative processes remotely.

Access to a more diverse set of people

In the past, when we tried to gather groups of people with different perspectives and experiences to come up with new ideas, we were limited to the people who happened to work in the same location.

What are the chances that the best minds in the world to solve your problem happen to share the same cafeteria or coffee machine that you do?

Remote teams enable us to connect to people in any location, to put together cross functional, international, and expert groups who have very different experiences, ideas, and perspectives.

This does not need to be confined to internal colleagues, we can more easily reach out to the world's best experts, to customers, and other partners to engage them in our process without the extensive travel time and cost needed to involve them in the past.

Many organizations are pursuing open innovation where they harness new start-ups, partners, and internal entrepreneurs to create new ideas, rather than just relying on their internal network of experts.

During 2020 at Global Integration, we created experience sharing web seminars with people from over 30 of our clients around the world. They shared their people's needs, challenges, and ideas and set up connections to help each other. We then facilitated small groups to work on specific themes. This led to several new training modules, including some of the content in this book. We got vital client input and willing participants to trial new training programs, and our clients got solutions completely adapted to what they needed. We would never have had the opportunity to get these people together physically.

These various partners in innovation are far more likely to engage over distance than to be available to travel to and meet in the same location.

Diversity of perspective and experience is extremely valuable in creativity and innovation and more likely to be available in a global virtual team than in a group of people who meet in the same bar every night.

Virtual collaboration tools bring opportunities to reduce creativity-inhibiting hierarchies and include introverts and other voices that may have been suppressed in a face-to-face conversation.

The basis of creativity is individual

Many of the concerns about organizing for creativity and innovation remotely stem from the belief that these are collective processes where we need to be face-to-face in a group to spark ideas and serendipity.

Where are you normally when you get your best ideas? Is it in a meeting?

Research shows that traditional meetings can stifle creativity due to anchoring and the impact of status and group think.

- Anchoring is when one idea is expressed, and it tends to influence all other ideas in one direction
- Power has an impact when a senior or influential member of the group expresses an opinion or supports an idea, and

this tends to inhibit lower status people from disagreeing or stating their own ideas

- Group think is where an idea or consensus evolves in a group and excludes other ways of thinking

In a meeting, when someone is talking, most people either stop thinking or are not listening.

Most people come up with their best ideas when they are alone, in the shower, on a walk or when focusing hard.

Faster and wider spread of ideas

The Internet and communication technologies were designed to reduce friction in communication. They cut the costs and barriers to connecting people and knowledge.

This should enable faster information exchange, questions, answers, and ideas among ever widening groups of people.

Today's digital networks increase the bandwidth, opportunity, and context for the exchange of ideas that might lead to something of value. Tools like Yammer and even Twitter enable ideas to be distributed widely and quickly and enable us to connect with others interested in and able to build on our ideas. Not all these suggestions will be helpful.

Fewer distractions, more creativity

Creative thinkers need time and space to think. They need to walk, meditate, listen to music, or stare off into space. All of these can be difficult in a traditional office. People working from home can control interruptions more easily and be more flexible on location and context.

Psychologist Mihaly Csikszentmihalyi has studied working in what he calls the flow state (see chapter above on designing your most productive and sustainable working pattern) and concluded that it is *very highly correlated with outstanding creative performance*.

The flow state is when we are concentrating and "in the zone", working on a clear, stretching goal with immediate feedback, where distractions are excluded, and time seems to fly.

It is hard to concentrate for long enough to achieve this state and do your best work in a busy office. Working from home can provide a good environment for achieving creative flow.

The research on the influence of remote work on creativity is limited. One study by economist E. Glenn Dutcher tested whether remote work productivity gains vary depending on the person and the nature of the task.

Researchers assigned two tasks to 125 students. The first was a simple repetitive task often used by psychologists to measure creativity. About half the participants did the task in a supervised lab, the other half remotely.

This small study indicated that people performed worse on routine (read boring) tasks and better on more creative tasks when working remotely. The researchers believed that this was because the creative tasks were more absorbing. People were more easily distracted from the routine tasks.

Hybrid workers are the most engaged and engagement improves innovation

A January 2020 Gallup survey found that engagement is highest when people spend some time working remotely and some time working in a location with their colleagues. The highest level of engagement for all employees was in people who worked 60% to 80% of their time off-site.

A 2015 report by Bailey, Madden, Alfes, and Fletcher consolidated the results of 214 academic studies. The combined findings showed a significant and unsurprising link between engagement and innovative work behavior.

Remote working improves engagement, and engagement improves innovation.

So what problems are we trying to solve?

With all this good news about the impact of remote working on creativity and innovation, you might be asking at this point what problem we are trying to solve. Are there specific aspects of creativity or innovation that do not work well in a remote context? Are there valid concerns we need to deal with, or are we just in the grip of some incorrect myths?

Does serendipity drive creativity and innovation?

Many concerns about organizing creativity and innovation remotely come from the perceived value of collective serendipity. Collective serendipity is when those chance meetings at the water cooler or over lunch lead to people combining ideas and sparking off each other to create great inventions.

A couple of questions to reflect on this

- What is the chance that the best people to solve a problem bump into each other at the right time in the same place?
- Were you been less innovative during the COVID-19 lockdowns when more people were working remotely? Many

organizations have reported the opposite with much faster innovation driven by the changing environment and ways of working

However, it is worth evaluating what role this really plays in creativity and innovation and which parts of serendipity we need to replicate virtually if we are going to work together remotely.

Serendipity is defined as "the fact of finding interesting or valuable things by chance". Bumping into others at the right time is only one of the mechanisms by which this might happen, and a random one at that. Can we really not do better than pure chance in organizing potentially valuable connections between people.

Here are the 7 top examples of serendipitous innovation identified by Wikipedia. As you read them, notice how many of them were generated by individuals rather than collectively?

1. The Post-It Note, which emerged after 3M scientist Spencer Silver produced a weak adhesive, and a colleague used it to keep bookmarks in place on a church hymnal

2. Silly Putty, which came from a failed attempt at synthetic rubber

3. The use of sensors to prevent automobile airbags from killing children, which came from a chair developed by the MIT Media Lab for a Penn and Teller magic show

4. The microwave oven. Raytheon scientist Percy Spencer first patented the idea behind it after noticing that emissions from radar equipment had melted the candy in his pocket

5. The Velcro hook-and-loop fastener, whose idea came about on a bird hunting trip when George de Mestral viewed under a

microscope the cockleburs stuck to his pants and saw that each burr was covered with tiny hooks

6. The Popsicle, whose origins go back to San Francisco where Frank Epperson, age 11, accidentally left a mix of water and soda powder outside to freeze overnight

7. The antibiotic penicillin, which was discovered by Sir Alexander Fleming after returning from a vacation to find that a Petri dish containing staphylococcus culture had been infected by a *Penicillium* mold, and no bacteria grew near it

Only two of these are not attributed to a specific individual who came up with the idea. It is not clear whether for numbers two and three the serendipitous idea came from an individual or a group.

None of them came from a chance encounter with another individual **during** the process of invention, although sometimes other individuals found different ways to apply the idea than the creator intended.

It appears that collective serendipity might not be as important as we might think. But we will give it the benefit of the doubt and assume there is some value in it. In that case, would not **intentional serendipity** be better than relying on chance meetings?

We will look at how to improve our chances of doing this virtually below.

Are some things just easier done face-to-face?

No technique works all the time. In important innovation projects, particularly in hybrid teams, it will be possible to have some face-to-face time available.

We should focus this scarce resource on things where being face-to-face seems to add the most value

- where there is conflict or disagreement about ideas
- where we need a group evaluation of ideas and commitment to the next steps
- maintaining relationships, people innovate best in an environment of trust and psychological safety, and this can often be built or reinforced faster through face-to-face interactions
- where we need to use laboratories, prototyping, and other physical facilities

Creativity and innovation techniques reimagined for remote and hybrid delivery

Here are some ideas on organizing for creativity when working remotely.

Increasing the probability of your individual serendipity

We can increase the chance of individual serendipity by exposing ourselves to a broader range of inputs, influences, and perspectives. Connect to thought leaders in your area of expertise through LinkedIn and Twitter. Seek out academic and popular articles for the topics you are interested in and summarize them.

As well as a specialized network on topics you are interested in, it is also useful having a broader "boundary spanning" network connecting you into different domains, areas of thought, and perspectives. Be careful about building a narrow bubble in which you only see opinions that already agree with your own.

Some organizations use co-working spaces and social office locations around their countries, allowing people to base themselves where they need to be based, but still have meaningful social interactions throughout the day.

In one survey of people who worked in co-working locations, 92% reported an increase in the size of their social circle since joining, while 80% reported an increase in the size of their business network.

It is also essential to communicate what you are working on. The more transparent you are about what you are working on and your areas of interest, the more likely someone will say, they can help.

"How can you be a thought leader if you do not tell people what you think?"

If you really want to take a topic area seriously, then you need to share your ideas to get ideas back. This is easier than ever before through platforms like social media and blogs.

Organizing for collective serendipity

We can increase the chance of collective serendipity when working remotely through planned spontaneous connections. In these events we

- have a clear statement of the problem or issue we want people to discuss
- invite a diverse audience with different perspectives around the areas to be discussed. If you need something very creative, this might include deliberately unusual choices such as involving musicians, librarians, and sports people as well as people from a range of functions, cultures, thinking styles, and perspectives

- seed the ideas – if we just let people have a random conversation, we are unlikely to get very far. We can create breakout areas or hold meetings around a particular theme that enables people to focus on solving a particular problem or discussing a particular opportunity or domain

- let interested people join the discussions they want to. By making the discussion areas voluntary, we attract people who have something to say or a passion about an area. It is unlikely that forced participants will be at their most creative

- allow some free association time where people share their initial ideas and the areas where they are working. Ideally, have someone capture this information on a mind map, or other application

- enable a parallel ideations process where individuals can capture their ideas and share them through chat or on an app like Miro or Mural. Let people work individually for a period and share ideas without any attempt to evaluate

- break into smaller virtual breakout groups of four to six people to focus more closely on the problem, review the ideas generated, and start to capture some themes and initial ideas. If you have more than one breakout group, rotate the membership so that people have a chance to interact with a broader range of others

- present the ideas back to the main group and give time for questions

- this may be enough on its own to create initial ideas and connections amongst people who would like to work together further on these ideas. If not, you can suggest some follow up groups and ask people to nominate themselves if they would like to be involved

A process like this must generate a higher probability of success than randomly bumping into someone in the queue of your cafeteria or at a water cooler.

Remote idea generation techniques

The objective at the idea generation phase of creativity and innovation is to generate as many ideas as possible without evaluation.

Ideally, this should be done individually. In a virtual meeting, they can be done individually in parallel. Give people a period of time to generate as many ideas as possible individually using the ideation techniques (below), and then quickly share with the group for later clustering and evaluation.

Here are some idea generation techniques you can use either individually or in virtual meetings

Reframing - this increases creativity by changing our interpretation or perception of something. By looking at it in a different way, we see new possibilities. Think about your problem through these different frames.

- **Different worlds** — could I use this object or idea in a different environment?

- **Learning from successes and mistakes** — what can I learn from this, even if it did not work?

- **Already solved** — what would it look like if I had already solved the problem? How else can I get to that stage? What journey would have got me there?

- **Silver lining** — what opportunities are lurking inside this problem?

- **Different perspectives** — how does this look to the other people involved?

- **What problem** – what if this was not a problem at all, but an improvement?

Another model for reframing is SCAMPER

- **Substitute** – find some part of your product or service you could replace with something different

- **Combine** – put together several ideas or products into a new whole – i.e., adding a camera to your phone

- **Adapt** – is there an idea already out there in another field that you could adapt to solve your problem

- **Modify** – change or exaggerate the situation to generate ideas

- **Put to another use** – try your existing ideas but apply them differently or to another area

- **Eliminate** – take out unnecessary processes and waste

- **Reverse** – do the opposite of the original purpose, idea, or way your product or service is used

Mind mapping

Mind mapping is a well-known technique that allows us to capture ideas and arrange them in a logical pattern. Mind mapping creates associations and makes the organization of ideas clearer.

There are many mind mapping apps we can use online, and these can be used to capture ideas and form associations in parallel by letting individuals add their ideas and tidying up later. This can be done live or asynchronously so people can add their ideas at a time convenient to them.

Changing your perspective

By deliberately choosing to look at a problem from a different perspective, we can radically increase the number of ideas about a problem or situation that we generate. This is easier to do if your group is already diverse as they bring their own different perspectives naturally.

A common technique for this is Edward de Bono's Six Thinking Hats. Each "hat" represents a different perspective. It is used during meetings or brainstorming sessions to stimulate team members to look at possible solutions from distinctly different perspectives or thinking directions.

During a creative session, every individual will spend some time looking at the issue from the perspective of each of the hats

- White hat – facts and information
- Red hat – feelings, intuitions, emotions, and hunches
- Black hats – judgment, legality, morality
- Yellow hat – optimism, benefits
- Green hat – new ideas, opportunities
- Blue hat – conclusions, action plans, next steps

Another perspective-changing tool is setting up your own virtual Advisory Board.

In this technique, you select people who you admire and who bring very different perspectives to the discussion. Imagine they are seated around the table advising you on your problem. Make sure the people you select bring a distinct and different perspective.

Come up with your own list. To illustrate the idea, how would these people solve your problem?

- Nelson Mandela
- Bill Gates
- Jeff Bezos
- Genghis Khan
- Thomas Edison

Another option is to create a random list of job titles; engineer, astronaut, orchestra conductor, Olympic sportsperson, fishing enthusiast, etc., and imagine, for example, what use they would get from your idea, product, or service. Changing your point of view will open many new areas of creativity.

You can use all these techniques individually or ask people to use them in your virtual meetings in parallel to generate more ideas.

Idea evaluation techniques

Once we have generated a lot of ideas, we now need to cluster, evaluate, and choose which ones to take forward.

Where groups really add value is in the evaluation of ideas and taking them forward to applications. You can use chat for this, or with larger groups, tools like Mural and Miro to simulate post-its on a large board.

It is usually necessary to cluster or combine ideas that are the same or similar in nature into groups. Because this takes time, it may be best to do this during a break in a virtual meeting, although there can be value in the discussions around which items are clustered together.

It is worth having a discussion around the most popular clusters to ensure there is a common understanding of what these mean.

We then normally have a voting system to choose the most popular ideas.

"Upvotes" work well online – participants register approval of or agreement with an idea through polling, adding an icon like a thumbs up to a comment, or using stickers on Zoom.

Simultaneous voting prevents anchoring or senior people from influencing the vote. Both can be a problem in face-to-face idea evaluation meetings, and once "winners" start to emerge, subsequent votes tend to reinforce this as groupthink emerges.

It is normal to limit the number of votes per participant so you will be more likely to get a clear result. A common method is to give people three to five votes to allocate to their top choices.

More scientifically, there is a formula to work out how many votes each person should have. The number of votes each = the number of options that are candidates to receive votes, divided by three. We do not know why this works, but it does.

Either of these approaches should produce a prioritized set of ideas. We then take the selected ideas forward for further work.

Once we reach this stage, we normally have something that we want to take forward for further development. This might be done by coordinating individuals in a star group or by more intensive spaghetti team working. At this point, our more general advice on virtual collaboration in previous chapters becomes relevant.

As with any crisis, COVID-19 has already sparked innovation. Roles and business models that relied on face-to-face contact have been quickly re-engineered. There has been a huge change even in traditionally slow to change areas such as the delivery of medical services and education through video.

The need for innovation will continue as we move into a tough economic situation in the aftermath.

Creativity and innovation are short term imperatives and also bring longer term opportunities.

Given our comments in this chapter, we do not believe that remoteness is a barrier to creativity and innovation if it is properly managed. It is more likely that remoteness will bring significant advantages.

Coaching questions

- How can we adapt the processes we use to manage creativity and innovation for the remote context?
- What advantages could working remotely bring, and how do we harness them?
- What will we continue to focus on face-to-face when we need innovation?

Part VI – Conclusions

Prediction is very difficult, especially if it is about the future **Niels Bohr**

It is too early to be certain about the longer-term effects of COVID-19 on the way we work.

In general, after a period of disruption, we continue to adopt the changes that made life better or easier. Where other things caused more friction in our lives or made things harder, we are keener to revert back to how we did things in the past.

Most organizations believe that a more flexible working pattern will be part of the way of working in the future for many more of their people. Remote and flexible working was already popular and growing before the pandemic, so it is very likely that this trend will accelerate.

Many individuals have enjoyed the flexibility and autonomy of working from home for the first time, though fewer want to do it every day.

Now is a good time to really think through what pattern of work is best for us as individuals and for our organizations. We certainly should not mindlessly flock back to the office without learning from this period and making changes. Neither can we continue to work from home without making some changes to make it sustainable for the long term.

This period gives us a real opportunity to develop a new, flexible, hybrid way of working where we combine the best of being in an office with the best of working from home. If we can find ways to integrate these ways of working, we have opportunities to improve productivity and engagement and reduce cost, and to make a significant impact on issues like carbon emissions and traffic congestion.

As we have seen, the challenge in doing this is not about the technology but about our behaviors, skills, way of working, and culture. It is by focusing on these that we can make remote and hybrid working better for nearly everyone. Here are some concluding thoughts on this.

Chapter 27. The community iceberg

On our face-to-face remote teams' programs, we often finish with a visualization exercise asking people to remember the best team they were ever part of. We then ask them to write down the one thing that made that peak experience of team working so successful for them personally.

We then ask them to stick their post-it note

- above a line on a flip chart if their one thing is about the **activity** of the team – the results, and the success they achieved.
- below the line if it is about the **community** of the team – the spirit, the people, energy, the fun

We call this exercise the "community iceberg" because most answers fit into the community section below the line consistently.

Usually, the team that people select was successful at delivering its activity, but what people remember is the relationships, the fun, and the energy of a great team.

I have learned that people will forget what you said, people will forget what you did, but people will never forget how you made them feel. Maya Angelou

It has been one of our mantras in our remote management training for many years to focus on "community before activity" but to be honest, in the past, in our training and in our books, we tended to leave the community message until the end.

It seemed to work better if we established our credibility by talking about collaboration, communication, and control which sound like the more tangible issues before we got onto the "fluffier stuff" around the community.

We believe (and hope) that one of the longer-term impacts of this difficult period on leadership will be to move the issue of community building and the human side of management and collaboration much higher up the leadership agenda.

If we focus too much on the results, we can sometimes damage the community that we need for sustained success. The results and deliverables of the team will also change constantly during your career.

Building a sense of community, fun, and team spirit is much more enduring. In virtual and hybrid teams, we are doing this in a new environment where we do not have so much face-to-face contact.

In the past, a lot of this community came as a free by-product of being in the same location. Today we will need to be much more intentional about it.

We have tried to build in community factors throughout the book this time, rather than leaving them to the end, but it is one of our concluding messages – focus on the community before activity.

Chapter 28. Connection's Consequences

It may seem that the changes we have been talking about are revolutionary, and for some organizations they are.

We have worked with many organizations over the last 25 years that have started to work in virtual teams. They usually find that this is the start of a journey towards a more integrated organization.

Here are some of the changes you will probably see emerging as you increase your amount of remote and hybrid working.

Closer integration and relationships with people in other locations

One of the trends that our participants have noticed already is that people are feeling much more connected to their colleagues in other locations and international operations.

Working from home has been a great leveler and has undermined the impact of distance.

Now that it is just as easy to connect with someone in a different continent as it is to connect to someone who used to work a few feet away, then why not connect with the best person, not just the closest.

More diverse voices being heard

Now that we do not have the difficult situation of several people clustered face-to-face in a room and a couple of others dialing in trying vainly to contribute, we have leveled the playing field and enabled a much more diverse group of voices to get involved.

Now that we can all contribute in parallel through chat and other engagement tools in online meetings, rather than fighting to be the person who speaks next, different voices are being heard.

As we mentioned in a previous chapter, remote teams give us some opportunities to increase both diversity and inclusion.

More international and cross-cultural working

As we get closer to our international colleagues and the difficulty of connecting internationally reduces, there will be an upsurge in interest in cross-cultural skills.

Cultural differences are something we immediately notice when we work with colleagues in other locations. It is useful to know a little about how to understand, enjoy, and reconcile these differences.

More matrix working

Virtual teams and organizations naturally become more integrated across the traditional silos of function and geography. It is just easier to connect with people now we are used to doing it virtually and traditional organizational boundaries become increasingly irrelevant.

Most of the organizations we have worked with have seen an increased use of virtual teams leading seamlessly into a more matrixed way of working.

Irrespective of whether you have a formal matrix organization structure or not, work increasingly cuts across boundaries and tends to become more lateral and horizontal. People reach out and connect with people who can answer their questions rather than those who have the right job title.

This conflicts with traditional ideas of control and hierarchy.

If you are experiencing this, you will find our book Making the Matrix Work useful.

Global talent will be more in demand and less locked up in local silos.

The best people will be at an increasing premium and will find it increasingly difficult to manage their workload as everyone wants them involved in their projects and teams.

If it no longer matters whether you are within driving distance of that expensive HQ office, then the pool of available labor becomes much wider.

But it goes both ways, if I am a highly talented employee based in Bangalore, Boston, Beijing, or Berlin, I will have my choice of working for organizations from any of these places and more.

Top talent always had a choice and, in the past, often exercised it by preferring to move to attractive city locations. These locations are much less attractive than they were.

People who were not mobile in the past would not be considered for some roles. Many more people will be able and open to a global virtual experience than those who were willing to physically uproot their families and move internationally.

It is the same for the best suppliers. In the past, at Global Integration, we occasionally lost work because, although we have people based around the world, we do not have an office in every city. Companies in markets like Australia were often reluctant to work with training suppliers who were not based in Australia. This makes sense when travel costs are a huge part of any project they agree with an international supplier. At the beginning of this year, a potential US customer for a global web seminar-delivered program decided to go with a local supplier "because they had an office in our city."

Since the lockdown, this has changed markedly. Organizations realize they will rarely if ever, be getting face-to-face with their suppliers in the short to medium term future, and location is becoming less of an issue.

This has been common in Europe for some time. In most sales interactions, there is little expectation from our clients that they need to get face-to-face. However, it seemed to be less accepted in the USA and Asia before the pandemic.

Today our trainers based in Europe can deliver web seminars early in the morning to Asia and later in the evening to the USA. Where they are based becomes unimportant. Our trainers based in Asia and the USA can offer the same flexibility. This gives us much more choice and flexible capacity. The deciding factors for clients are the quality of the content and the ability of the facilitator to create engagement and interaction, not where they happen to work from.

Now expand this on a global scale. Any organization with access to the Internet can access the world's best talent and the world's best suppliers, irrespective of location.

We expect this will lead to a polarized market with the absolute top global talent and top global suppliers taking a disproportionate share of the benefits. It is no time to be average or a generalist dabbling in a subject when companies have much more choice and can go straight to the global leaders.

People will get used to more autonomy and demand more control

Individuals working from home value and need higher levels of autonomy and flexibility and will expect this to continue. This will change their attitude to being managed and their desire for higher levels of self-direction.

Traditional managers will find they have fewer tools to resist this development now that people have demonstrated that it can work. Those organizations that fight a rear-guard action insisting on their people returning to the office full time will find attracting and retaining the best people difficult.

Even where we are able to get back to a face-to-face working environment, employees will want more flexible ways of working. We are already hearing that candidates in recruitment interviews are asking what a flexible future working process will look like.

From what we have seen in other organizations, the changes above will be largely positive developments, leading to higher levels of empowerment and engagement and better performance.

We hope you will find this book useful in helping you design a system of work that is better for you as an individual and better for your organization. Remote and hybrid working can make organizations more cost-effective and attractive to work for and make a big difference in individual productivity and engagement.

To make this sustainable for the long term, we need to concentrate on our new ways of working.

We would love to hear your experiences or challenges in implementing the ideas from the book. You can contact us through our website www.global-integration.com or find us on social media.

If we can help you through training or consulting, you know where we are.

We wish you good luck.
Kevan and Alan

Please leave a review

Reviews are very important to the success of online books. If you have enjoyed this book, please leave a (hopefully 5-star) review wherever you bought it from.

Reviews make the book visible to more people and help us get the message out.

If you have any suggestions for improvement, you can send them to us direct at europe@global-integration.com

Thank you for your help.

Get more support

Our company Global Integration inspires and enables people to succeed in increasingly connected organizations.

We specialize in

- Remote, virtual, working from home and hybrid team working
- Matrix management
- Agile and Digital Leadership

We developed the world's first remote teams training over 25 years ago and have trained over 150,000 people in more than 400 major organizations around the world in these skills.

We have been running interactive web seminars for 15 years and bring deep expertise and global capability to both the content and delivery of remote learning.

If you liked the ideas in this book, you will love our training. We run highly interactive face-to-face workshops and online web seminars on all of the topics in the book and more.

You can run these as bite sized sessions for your individual team or as part of a more comprehensive learning path for your whole organization.

We have trainers based around the world.

You can sample our ideas in our books and free videos and web seminars on remote, matrix and agile working at

www.global-integration.com

Other books by Kevan Hall and Alan Hall

Kill Bad Meetings – **transform your culture, improve collaboration, and accelerate decisions.**

This book will show you how to halve the number of meetings you attend and improve the quality of the ones that remain.

"Both thought-provoking and actionable. In just a few hours we identified opportunities to reduce the number of meetings and the number of people in meetings. Within 24 hours we have reduced complexity, increased efficiency and lifted engagement". Sally Cairns, Chief People Officer, Paddy Power Betfair

Making The Matrix work – **how matrix managers engage people and cut through complexity**

As work becomes more horizontal, cutting across the traditional silos of function and geography, many of us are now working in a more matrixed way in multiple teams, with multiple stakeholders, and sometimes with more than one boss. This book helps you develop the matrix mindset and skill set. Succeed in a world where higher levels of ambiguity, accountability without control, and influence without authority are the norm.

"A much-needed look at managing and leading in complex modern organizations. Practical tools you can implement to speed up your company". Bob Morton, Head of People Development Competence Center, Europe-MEA, Ciba Specialty Chemicals

<u>Speed Lead</u> – **faster, simpler ways to manage people, projects, and teams in complex companies**

When companies grow, they become more complex, but this complexity eventually makes them slower, more expensive to run, and less satisfying to work for. This practical book can save you a day a week and accelerate the delivery of results by showing you practical steps you can take to cut out unnecessary cooperation, communication, and control.

"We want our companies to be faster, simpler and easier to run – this refreshing blend of challenging ideas and practical tools shows us how." Karl Kahofer, Group president Europe and Asia Pacific, Rubbermaid/Irwin

Dedication

We wrote this book in the second half of 2020. A year where organizations and individuals learned a lot about each other.

We would like to dedicate this book first to all to our colleagues at Global Integration. Our central people, who were largely new to working from home, never missed a beat, moving our training programs (already 50% virtual) to 100% virtual in a matter of days and providing superb service in a challenging year.

Our remote people, used to working from home, stepped up to train thousands of people around the world on how to cope with their sudden new way of working. We stuck to our values, providing free video resources to many thousands of people through social media and free training sessions for our clients who did not have the ability to pay. We would like to give a special mention to Tony Poots in his 25th year with Global Integration. He has been a massive part of our success.

We would also like to thank our clients, who continued to invest in and support their people and trusted us to deliver. Dozens of them also worked closely with us to co-create new programs that met their needs during a unique period. Our shared experiences around the world brought us closer.

We would also like to thank our participants for their stories, their engagement, and their good humor throughout. We felt a massive desire from them this year to share experiences, connect, and learn.

Finally, of course, thanks to our families and especially our wives Diane and Jess! We spent a lot of time together this year. It is a good job we are so easy to have around!

Thank you all.
Kevan and Alan

Made in the USA
Monee, IL
11 April 2021